FEMINIST FRAMEWORKS
Building Theory on Violence Against Women

LISA S. PRICE

FERNWOOD PUBLISHING • HALIFAX

Editing: Anne Griffiths
Cover photo: courtesy of Pamela Sleeth
Printed and bound in Canada by: Hignell Printing Limited

A publication of:
Fernwood Publishing
Site 2A, Box 5, 32 Oceanvista Lane
Black Point, Nova Scotia, B0J 1B0
and 324 Clare Avenue
Winnipeg, Manitoba, R3L 1S3
www.fernwoodbooks.ca

Fernwood Publishing Company Limited gratefully acknowledges
the financial support of the Department of Canadian Heritage,
the Nova Scotia Department of Tourism and Culture
and the Canada Council for the Arts for our publishing program.

Library and Archives Canada Cataloguing in Publication

Price, Lisa S. (Lisa Sydney), 1955-
Feminist frameworks : building theory on violence against women / Lisa Price.

Includes bibliographical references.
ISBN 1-55266-157-1

1. Women--Violence against. 2. Abusive men. 3. Feminist theory. I. Title.

HV6250.4.W65P725 2005   362.88'082   C2005-900925-X

CONTENTS

ACKNOWLEDGEMENTS

This book began life as a chapter in my PhD thesis. In the birth of that work, I am especially indebted to two intellectual midwives, Jalna Hanmer and Gabriele Griffin. They coached, advised, counselled and critiqued that work to its eventual entry into the world. For this current work, I am indebted to Jalna for the materials and comments she provided regarding "john schools."

Thank you to Kim Goodliffe for first recommending I approach Fernwood with the book proposal. At Fernwood, my editor Lydia Perovic first recognized the potential for creating a Basics book out of the kernel of the PhD chapter. I also appreciate Lydia for her patience with my slowness in writing. Anne Griffiths provided a careful reading of the draft text. Her skill and attention made for a much better book, for which I am grateful.

Karen Boyle, Kevin Davison and the librarians at Gibsons Public Library were all invaluable in tracking down research materials for me. I am also indebted to Karen and Kevin for their unflagging support and belief in me and for their critical reflections on parts of the manuscript.

My family, Martha and Angela, provided the psychic space which allowed me to work but also frequently reminded me of the need for balance between writing and the rest of my life. Martha was also invaluable in applying her keen eye to the revision process. Finally, Tara Pigott, Timothy Hayward and Paul Termansen each in their own way helped me sustain equilibrium during this writing process.

INTRODUCTION

> I know only two things for certain. One is that we gain nothing by walking around the difficulties and merely indulging in wishful thinking. The other is that there is always something one can do oneself. In the most modest form, this means: to study, to try to sort out different proposals and weigh the effect of the proposed solutions—even if they are only partial solutions. Otherwise there would be nothing left but to give up. And it is unworthy of human beings to give up. (Alva Myrdal quoted in Bok 1991: 286)

On December 6, 1989, Marc Lépine[1] entered the engineering school of L'Ecole Polytechnique in Montreal carrying an assault rifle. In a classroom he separated the men from the women and shouting "You are all feminists," began to shoot. Lepine killed fourteen young women before turning the gun on himself.

How do we make sense of an event such as the Montreal Massacre? Or wife battering or war rape? What does making sense mean in the context of violence against women? Political philosopher Hannah Arendt, describing what prompted her to write *The Origins of Totalitarianism* in the immediate aftermath of the Holocaust, argues that the outrageous requires not only lamentation and denunciation but also comprehension (1979: xiv). She goes on to suggest that comprehension requires a kind of intellectual courage, a determined willingness to bear the burden of events, to face facts unflinchingly.

For thirty-five years now, feminists of the contemporary women's movement have worked to identify issues of violence against women, to provide services to the women and children victimized by men's violence and to fight for change in the legal, social, economic and ideological conditions that allow such violence to proliferate. These three aspects of feminists' work—identification, service provision and activism—are related particularly inasmuch as they all have a common grounding in women's lives. Feminists start by listening to women, to what they say about their experience in the past, their needs in the present and their hopes for the future.

Based on what they were hearing from women, feminists named rape as a crime of sexual violence against women, founded rape crisis centres and lobbied endlessly for changes in laws and changes in police and legal procedures. So too have feminists listened to and spoken out on women's experience of wife assault, sexual harassment in the workplace, child sexual abuse and dating violence. Feminists have also exposed systems of pornography and prostitution as woman abuse and are investigating the prevalence and meaning of elder abuse.

Through all this work, feminists have learned a great deal about men's violence against women and children. Sometimes it seems we know too much; the horror is so much, so various, so unrelenting, so unthinkable. But of course it is thinkable, and we have an obligation to think it and speak it and continue to struggle to end it.

We have also learned about women's courage and determination and creativeness in overcoming the effects of male violence. We have learned that individual women do survive, that they do emerge from experiences of violence and degradation strong and knowledgeable and whole. We have learned that women can and do make the transition from victim to survivor. Women do it every day.

Before proceeding further, I should at least briefly discuss who "we" are. For the purposes of this book, feminists (and pro-feminist men) share an analysis of women's oppression by men which is pan-historical and cross-cultural. Oppression exists in all social realms including the political, the economic and the legal. It is present in our smallest and most intimate relations and in the largest institutions of the state. It is present in all life stages, from the sexual abuse of toddlers to the feminization of poverty among our elder citizens. As shall be discussed more fully in the body of the text, feminists recognize that gender oppression acts dynamically with other axes of oppression such as race, ethnicity, class, citizenship, sexuality and physical and mental ability/disability. Feminists are committed to being a force for change in women's interests.

Feminism is also a method of analysis, a standpoint, a way of looking at the world from the perspective of women. It questions government policies, popular culture, ways of doing and being, and asks how women's lives are affected by these ideological and institutional practices. Feminism recognizes a unity among women, recognizes that we all live somewhere on a continuum of oppression with none of us completely free of male dominance. While cognizant of differences both individual and social, feminists understand that to work for women is to work for ourselves.

A note on terminology may be in order here. There is some debate among feminist thinkers regarding the appellations applied to women who have experienced male violence. In particular, some theorists maintain that it is important for women to overcome understanding themselves as victims of male violence. It is important for women to make the transition from victim to survivor. As I have written:

> The stories of men's violence are also stories of women's survival. Women do survive in the literal sense: they outlive the violence done to them. They do what Linda Marchiano did: they endure while they have to, escape when they can, and live beyond the violence. Alone and with the support of feminist services such as transition houses, women find ways to overcome the consequences

of what has been done to them. (1989: 96)

MacKinnon, on the other hand, argues:

> For example, the parade of horrors demonstrating the systematic victimization of women often produces the criticism that for me to say women are victimized reinforces the stereotype that women "are" victims, which in turn contributes to their victimization. If this stereotype is a stereotype, it has already been accomplished, and I come after. To those who think "it isn't good for women to think of themselves as victims," and thus seek to deny the reality of their victimization, how can it be good for women to deny what is happening to them? Since when is politics therapy? (1987: 220)

It may be possible to reconcile the two positions by adding in a temporal component, that is, in the immediate aftermath of, say, a sexual assault it seems important to emphasize the women's victimhood. But in the longer term it may be necessary for the victim to make the transition to survivor.

As to the permanent potential of male violence Elizabeth Stanko writes: "All women have some experience of male violation.... *To walk the streets warily at night is how we actually feel our femininity*" (1985: 157, italics in original). Similarly, Lori Heise maintains, "There are two experiences that unite women across culture and class, those of giving birth and the fear of male violence" (quoted in Hotaling 1996: 1). This may be somewhat overblown but the point for both Stanko and Heise, it seems to me, is that men's violence is so pervasive that virtually none of us live free from it, even if we do not always consciously pay attention to it.

As I sit alone in my study in the summer of 2004, I imagine who you the readers of this book will be and what will prompt you to open it. I assume you are looking for a concise introduction to specifically feminist analyses of issues of violence against women. You want to make sense of child sexual abuse or sexual harassment or more generally the violence men do to women and you hope/believe an overtly feminist text offers the best available resource in your quest. Most of all you are looking for a grounding. I project these wishes on you because they are ones I have experienced for years, and while I certainly do not promise that this one book will answer all of your questions, it is intended to be a guide to the literature, a signpost to where you might look for more information and analysis. In short, this book is an *entrée* to a much larger field of texts.

As to why readers would be searching for such a text, I imagine that the motives will vary greatly. Some will be looking to make sense of their own direct and indirect experiences of men's violence. Other women who as yet have not been confronted by violent men, at least not in their conscious memory, may be eager to learn from other women's experiences.

More than that, though, I would claim that an education in feminism is incomplete without a nuanced understanding of the role of violence in the lives of women and men. This is the "feminism unmodified" of which MacKinnon writes. Or, in Cole's words,

> It was the issue of violence against women that gave radical feminism its spark, and what distinguished radical feminism from its sister groups. By naming what was happening to women, by using terms that had not made their way into public consciousness, let alone public policy, radical feminists tugged away at public awareness until the unspoken came out of its closet. We talked about rape, violence against women in the home, sexual harassment and more recently about incest. As activists and sociologists tried to make sense of the crisis, feminist research, the kind that listened to women, uncovered the truth that sexual abuse was epidemic, not occasional, more normal than marginal. (1995: 215–16)

I at one time worked for the Women's Research Centre, a national feminist organization based in Vancouver. For each research project, when it came time to write up our results, we would ask each other, "Who is sitting on your shoulder?" The question was meant in part to help the writer bring into focus the audience for whom she was writing. It was also meant to keep at the forefront of our minds the women whose lives we hoped would benefit from the work we did. For this current project who sat on my shoulders were some of the undergraduate Women's Studies students I used to teach. They were on fire, desperate for knowledge and analysis to rebut the image of women they got from their other courses. They wanted to know everything all at once. Their passion, their demands for knowledge and analysis were sometimes frightening but also made the students a joy to teach. I felt very privileged to be their instructor. So I imagine with this book women (and a few men) will want a concise overview of feminist understandings (in the plural) of violence against women. The book is an introduction to a large body of work (witness the bibliography). Here the readers will meet some of the most prominent thinkers on the question of male violence—Susan Brownmiller and Catherine MacKinnon and Susan Cole and all the rest. Whether university/college students or not, readers have a hunger for which this book is simply an *hors-d'oeuvre*.

It will shortly become apparent that a number of texts I cite date from the 1980s and in a few cases the 1970s. They are included as foundational texts upon which much feminist theorizing has been built. Furthermore, some of the insights contained in these texts remain as fresh today as when they were first written. In short, early works by Brownmiller, Hanmer, and Dobash and Dobash remain crucial to the project of making sense of male violence against women.

I have called this book *Feminist Frameworks* because I envision it providing you the readers with a structure within which you might develop your own analyses of men's violent, intimidating and coercive behaviours toward women and children. It is the frame upon which you will build the walls and doors and windows of your particular conceptual house. I hope you will find that the frameworks presented here are not idiosyncratic but are built on a firm substratum of thirty years of feminist writing on male violence.

This book constitutes a literature review of texts on the origins, operations and meanings of violence against women. It is not an exhaustive search. It is limited in the first instance to widely available published materials, which, given the feminist movement's activist history and commitment to *praxis*, is a significant if unavoidable limitation. Perhaps more critically, the review is restricted to materials published in English, thereby overlooking substantial bodies of work. These circumscriptions are not unrelated. With notable exceptions such as Nawal el Sadaawi's *The Hidden Face of Eve* and Rigoberta Menchu's *I, Rigoberta*, few feminist texts are available in translation in the English-speaking world. Put simply, what is published in the English-speaking world tends to be what is written in English.[2]

Even with these limitations, there is a large and rather daunting array of works. In the end, the choice of which writers and which texts to include in this review is based in part on an assessment of the significance of contributions—writings that pushed our thinking along—together with a wish to avoid repetition. Thus, for example, of Diana Russell's numerous books on rape, I have included only one: *Rape in Marriage* is at once representative of Russell's larger *oeuvre* and historically noteworthy as the first extensive analysis of wife rape.

I have chosen to discuss individual writers and texts rather than schools, either national (British, American, Canadian) or political (liberal, socialist, radical feminist). While it is sometimes important to note the national context of a work, particularly when discussing law and law reform, by and large it seems similarities outweigh differences to the extent that identifying "British feminism," for example, simply is not useful. Similarly, classifications of feminist theory too often lead, as Anne Edwards points out, to oversimplification and distortion (1987: 15). Where appropriate, writers have been grouped thematically as sharing a common perspective on particular issues. That said, readers will find that the majority of writers included in this book tend to the radical stream of feminism, though some liberal feminists are also included. This is not deliberate on my part; rather, when I came to examine the metanarratives of men's violence against women, I found that it was the radical feminists (as opposed to, say, socialist or psychoanalytic feminists) who had the most to say. Finally, the book examines feminist analyses in eight broad areas:

definitions of violence; theories on the origins of male sex/sexual violence; Catharine MacKinnon's critique of sex and sexuality; intersectionality and violence against women; violence as process; choice and accountability; feminist interventions into the violence process; and feminist jurisprudence. When viewed together, these streams of thought offer a comprehensive, though not exhaustive, *précis* of the work undertaken to date to explain men's violence against women.

NOTES

1. Some feminists argue that Lepine's name should not be broadcast and that instead the names of his victims should be remembered. I take the view that perpetrators should be recognized as the ordinary men they are. Accordingly, I use Lepine's name but also include the names and brief biographies of his victims in Appendix I.

2. In Canada some government-supported feminist research organizations such as the Canadian Association for the Advancement of Women publish all materials in both official languages. Independent feminist publishing houses by and large lack the financial resources to do so. Journals such as *Resources for Feminist Research/Documentation sur la recherche feministe* publish individual articles in either English or French but only the abstracts are translated.

1. Defining Violence

Telling the truth is not blaming. It is telling the truth.
(Sonia Johnson 1987: 22)

Why is it still a political statement to refer to *male* violence against women, rather than to "private" violence?
(Elizabeth Stanko 1985: 161)

The preeminent feminist contribution to our understanding of violence is that violence is gendered. In other words, there is a clear gender division between those who do violence and those who suffer it. This does not mean that women are inherently incapable of violence. Nor does it mean that men and boys are never victims. Rather, it means that when we look at statistics on rape, battering, child sexual abuse, pornography, prostitution, sexual harassment, stalking, sexual murder and other forms of "personal" violence, the inescapable fact is that overwhelmingly the perpetrators are men and the victims are women and girls.

This recognition remains contested in some segments of popular culture. Speaking of male violence is called "blaming men"; it is "political," often in the dismissive sense. More subtly, bureaucratic, political and academic discourses often maintain what appears to be a willful blindness to the gendered nature of violence. The description given by Mary MacLeod and Esther Saraga of the silence surrounding the causes of child sexual abuse is illustrative:

Why then is there evident in political, professional and journalistic writings, such a curious absence of discussion on why abuse occurs? The answer should come as no surprise to feminists; it enables an avoidance of the most glaring feature of child sexual abuse: it is something that, overwhelmingly, men do to children. The men come from every social class, and from all kinds of families and cultures; they are brothers, uncles, baby-sitters, friends, strangers, grandfathers, stepfathers, and fathers. They have in common that they are men, but little else that we know. (1988: 16–17)

Susan Griffin's 1971 article (reprinted in 1978) , "Rape: The All-American Crime," is commonly cited as the first widely disseminated statement on the maleness of violence. Many of the themes she touches on, such as the inseparability of male sexuality and violence in some cultures (1978: 317), continue to be developed by feminist theorists today. I shall discuss these themes in more detail later in this book. For now, the point to be stressed is this: for all of the writers considered in this review, gender is foundational to the definition of violence. Whatever debates and disagreements may arise, unanimity exists in the claim that the subject is properly named "male violence" or "men's violence."

The question of whether the term "violence" should be restricted to the exercise of physical force seems to depend upon context. An early opponent of this position is Jalna Hanmer. Writing in 1978 she argues that a "sociological" definition of violence must include not only the use of force but also its threat. She bases this argument on an instrumentalist view of violence, that is, inasmuch as either the use of force or the threat of force serves to "compel or constrain women to behave or not to behave in given ways" (1978: 220), both constitute violence.

Writing sixteen years later, Anne Jones quotes Emerge, a Boston counselling program for men who batter: "Violence *need not involve physical contact with the victim*, since intimidating acts like punching walls, verbal threats, and psychological abuse can achieve the same result" (1994: 88). Jones herself then comments, "Behaviour you might not think of as 'violence,' behaviour you might think of merely as getting things off your chest ... *is* violence if it coerces or frightens another person" (1994: 88).[1]

Dorie Klein and Jill Radford further expand the definition of violence, encompassing not only physical force, threat and coercion, but also, it would seem, any preventable harm. Klein, writing about nineteenth-century gynecological practice, states: "These women and the generations who followed them into dangerous operations and involuntary childbearing are as much the victims of violence as the woman raped in the street by a stranger" (1981: 69). In Radford's introduction to an anthology of essays on femicide (the killing of women *qua* women), she states:

> In this era of AIDS, femicide includes the deliberate transmission of the HIV virus by rapists. The concept of femicide also extends itself beyond legal definitions of murder to include situations in which women are permitted to die as a result of misogynous attitudes or social practices. (1992: 7)

Other writers are more constrained in their application of the term violence. Elizabeth Stanko, for example, indicates that though a wide range of actions may be harmful to women, only those involving physical force are properly termed "violence."

R. Emerson Dobash and Russell Dobash are even more restrictive. Their definition of wife battering is limited to "the persistent direction of physical force against a marital partner or cohabitant" (1979: 11). This definition stands in opposition to the many analysts for whom wife battering includes a series of abuses such as psychological torment, economic control and/or deprivation, social isolation and familial estrangement.

I am inclined to favour this restrictive application of the definition of violence for the simple reason that a term limitlessly expanded becomes meaningless. Unwanted childbearing, whether enforced by a husband or by the state, denies women their bodily integrity and autonomy. As such it is harmful. Threat and coercion serve to control women's behaviour and violate the right of autonomous action, and so are harmful. Psychological abuse is a form of mistreatment. But in the absence of the exercise of physical force, I hesitate to call these harms and violations *violence*, preferring Stanko's "listing" approach, that is, to speak of behaviour which is "violent, intimidating, coercive, indeed damaging to women" (1985: 4).

Context is important here. Consider, for example, some feminist definitions of rape. Lorenne Clark and Debra Lewis describe rape as "sexual intercourse accomplished through the use or threat of force" (1977: 164). Russell distinguishes rape by force, rape by threat of force and rape "when the [woman] is in no position to consent because she is unconscious, drugged, asleep, or in some other way helpless" (1982: 43). Finally, in her work on fraternity gang rape (the rape of female students on campus by groups of male fraternity members), Peggy Reeves Sanday argues that rape occurs whenever a woman refuses or is incapable of giving consent to sexual activity. Like Russell and Clark and Lewis, she specifies that acquiescence in response to coercion does not constitute consent. Sanday goes further, though, in her rendering of coercion, when she argues that:

> Coercion need not be accomplished by physical force or threat of force but may be inherent in the circumstances surrounding the transaction. The circumstances in which a single female is in the company of a half dozen drunken males on their premises who demand that she engage in sex with them are inherently coercive. (1990: 15–16)

If we are to retain the restrictive definition of violence as the exercise of physical force in this context, then we must distinguish violent and non-violent rape—surely an untenable stance. Similarly, inasmuch as some men who sexually abuse children rely more on authority and persuasion than on physical force, are we to say molestation is not a form of violence? According to Judith Herman:

> Because a child is powerless in relation to an adult, she is not free to refuse a sexual advance. Therefore, any sexual relationship between the two must necessarily take on some of the coercive characteristics of rape.... The question of whether force is involved is largely irrelevant, since force is rarely necessary to obtain compliance. The parent's authority over the child is usually sufficient to compel obedience. (1981: 27)

Sensitivity to context provides one solution to this problem, if a paradoxical one. When we speak of *issues* such as rape and wife battering, it seems appropriate to do so under the general rubric of "violence against women." When, on the other hand, we wish to describe *specific behaviours* that cause harm to women, we may be better served demarcating physical force, threat, intimidation, coercion, abuse of authority, etc. Hence "violence" may be a general category *or* a specific action depending upon the context.

Many feminist theorists have pointed to the power of naming as crucial to the maintenance of male hegemony (see, for example, Dworkin 1981; Frye 1983; and Price 1988). In the area of violence against women, a number of writers observe that definitions of violence, especially legal definitions, are based on men's perceptions of what harms women, rather than on women's experiences. For example, until recently, child sexual abuse was legally defined as statutory rape, requiring evidence of full vaginal penetration. The sexual abuse of boy children went unrecognized by law. The only harm recognized in this definition is the loss of virginity. From the perspective of victims, this loss—if it occurs at all—is not the only or even most significant harm done to them.

In response to the dissonance of men's perception and women's experience, some writers, including Susan Brownmiller, argue that what is needed is a "female definition" (1975: 18) of crimes such as rape. In essence, the argument is that by shifting authority from men to women, we will achieve a truer picture of what these crimes are. This argument may be valid, but its practical accomplishment is problematic. How are "female definitions" to be arrived at? How do we reach consensus among women; whose voices, whose experiences should serve as the basis of our definitions?

Liz Kelly's approach is to individualize self-definition. Rather than seeking a universal women's definition, she says we should regard sexual violence against women as any act which "is experienced by the woman or girl, at the time or later, as a threat, invasion, or assault" (1988: 41).[2] Thus the same act may be understood as violence when experienced by one woman and not violence when experienced by another.

Such an approach may be difficult to codify legally. More importantly, though, it creates analytic problems for feminists, seen most clearly in the case of child sexual abuse. Many children lack the knowledge or cognitive development to understand that what is being done to them is abuse. Additionally, some abusers, intent on gaining a child's collusion, couple abuse with affection, or they stimulate their victims to orgasm. In such cases, the children do not necessarily subjectively experience abuse; they experience "love," perhaps "pleasure." Similarly, though less extremely, many raped women and battered women express feelings of ambivalence—even acceptance—about what has been done to them. If a battered woman says, "I didn't know it was abuse," does that mean it was not? It would appear Kelly's approach anticipates this problem inasmuch as she acknowledges that experience may be retroactive. But the appearance has no substance, for it amounts to only a temporal shift. An adult, reflecting on her childhood experience of sexual abuse, may come to comprehend the violence done to her. Equally, she may not. A battered woman may not ever term her experience as battering.

Jill Radford, writing in favour of Kelly's definition, opines that it is "consistent with one of the basic tenets of feminism—women's right to name our experience" (1992: 3). Respect for individual women *is* fundamental to feminism. But respect and agreement are not the same thing. More critically, given that the task of feminist theory is to develop a general analysis of women's oppression, individual subjectivity may seem an insubstantial ground upon which to build social definitions.

Supplanting men's definitions of violence against women is a vitally important project, which need not be abandoned merely on the basis of methodological difficulties. While *individual* subjectivity may not be sufficient to the task of creating social definitions, perhaps *collective* subjectivity is. This brings us back to Brownmiller's notion of female definitions. If we begin with an understanding that knowledge, meaning and consciousness are not objects but social processes, then we can imagine a course by which feminists may arrive at a broad consensus on social definitions of violence against women.

The procedure I have in mind will be familiar to any who have engaged in feminist qualitative research. It is a matter of gathering many individual stories, applying to them judgement and analysis, and submitting the resulting general description to public discussion and debate. Repeated at many sites over time, this process draws us ever closer to understandings of violence reflective of women's experiences (rather than men's perceptions), which have the authority of commonality and critique. It is, in short, a means by which we may avoid the twin pitfalls of arguments of false consciousness and epistemic liberalism.[3] The key is that women's experiences of men's violence are collectivized and politicized. This is sometimes referred to as "feminist standpoint epistemology."

Earlier in this chapter I noted that all of the writers here considered take the gendered nature of violence to be foundational to their analysis. Interestingly, in spite of this unanimity only a few writers go on to explore the theoretical significance of gendered violence. Kathleen Barry, for example, defines crimes against women as "those acts of violence which are directed at women because of their female sexual definition" (1985: 164), by which one understands her to mean women's role as the objects and satisfiers of male sexual desire. For Dorie Klein, the issue goes beyond sexuality. She says that pan-historically and cross-culturally, "women have often been injured *as women:* as childbearers, sexual objects for men, and nurturers" (1981: 64). Jane Caputi and Diana Russell see an analogy between gendered and racialized violence. As they argue:

> Lépine's murders were hate crimes targeting victims by gender, not race, religion, ethnicity or sexual orientation.... Most people today understand that lynchings and pogroms are forms of politically motivated violence, the objectives of which are to preserve white and gentile supremacy. Similarly, the goal of violence against women—whether conscious or not—is to preserve male supremacy. (1992: 14)

What each of these writers is describing is the targeting of women because they are women. I call this targeting "sex violence." Analogous to sex discrimination, sex violence encapsulates the pattern of women and girls becoming the objects of male violence because they are female. Socially, being female means being vulnerable, being subordinate and, at least sometimes, being the object of hate. As Radford, in a discussion of femicide comments, "while men are murdered more frequently than women, men are rarely murdered simply because they are men" (1992: 10). That women are killed because they are women Radford calls "misogynous" (1992: 3).

And is this sex violence also sexual violence? Sexuality is a pivotal problematic for feminist theorists, especially in relation to violence. Broadly speaking, there are two conceptual approaches to the issue: first, that crimes such as rape are best understood as "violence *not* sex"; second, that "violence *is* sex." In reviewing arguments in favour of the "violence *not* sex" conceptualization, a number of discrete but interrelated themes emerge. Most basically, there is a disavowal of the presence of sexuality or sexual motivation in crimes of violence against women. Klein, Herman, Sanday and Sheffield all in various ways adopt this position. Klein writes that "rape is not an erotic act" (1981: 71). On the subject of fraternity gang rape, Sanday claims "the sexual act is not concerned with sexual gratification" (1990: 10). Similarly, Herman claims sexual pleasure is not the primary motivation in cases of incest (1981: 87–88). And Sheffield sees sexual harassment as analogous to rape "in that it is less an expression of sexuality than of power" (1987: 180).

Power, dominance and control constitute the second theme that emerges. In rejecting sexuality as a cause for violence, the writers cited in the above paragraph all go on to identify the desire for and expression of dominance as the principal incitement to crimes against women. Sanday's comment is representative: "The sexual act is not concerned with sexual gratification but with the deployment of the penis as a concrete symbol of masculine social power and dominance" (1990: 10). Radford, in her femicide work, makes a similar claim (1992: 3). Some writers see assaults including rape and child sexual abuse as expressions of hostility, aggression and sometimes even fear. Herman, for example, argues that incest can be seen as "an expression of hostility to all women" and that a daughter is targeted simply because she is perceived by the perpetrator as "the woman least capable of retaliation" (1981: 87–88). Brownmiller suggests that rapists see women as "hated person[s]" (1975: 185). These three themes—the denial of sexual content, the primacy of the desire for power as motivation and hostility as an ancillary motive—are summarized most succinctly in a quotation from Klein, who says, "One must understand that at bottom rape is not an erotic act at all. It is an act of violent domination, cloaking hatred and fear" (1981: 71).

Another explanatory theme within the "violence *not* sex" stream is that of women as property. Brownmiller's rendering of the motivations for rape best exemplifies this theme and its relation to those previously discussed. According to Brownmiller:

> Like assault rape is an act of physical damage to another person, and like robbery it is also an act of acquiring property: the intent is to 'have' the female body in the acquisitory meaning of the term. A woman is perceived by the rapist both as hated person and desired property. Hostility *against her and possession* of her may be simultaneous motivations, and the hatred for her is expressed in the same act that is the attempt to 'take' her against her will. In one violent crime, rape is an act against person and property. (1975: 185)

Clark and Lewis also point to sexual property acquisition as a motive element in rape; however their argument is rather more nuanced than Brownmiller's. Whereas Brownmiller looks at the perceptions of the rapist, Clark and Lewis gaze more broadly to encompass historically existing juridical and popular conceptions of rape as a property crime. They argue:

> Rape is simply theft of sexual property under the ownership of someone other than the rapist.... From the beginning, rape was perceived as an offence against property, not as an offence against the person on whom the act was perpetrated, and it has not lost the shrouds of these historical origins. (1977: 116)

Clark and Lewis go on to argue that legally treating rape as distinct from other forms of assault only serves to enshrine the notion of women as property. They write:

> A sexual attack is, in itself, neither better nor worse than any other kind of attack.... To treat rape as a sexual offence simply because it involves a penis and a valuable vagina, only reinforces the connections between women as property and women's sexuality as the source of their property value. (1977: 179)

This quotation contains the last major theme in the "violence *not* sex" argument; namely, that sexual assaults are neither experientially nor actually different from other assaults. Clark and Lewis are the strongest—though certainly not the only—proponents of this theme. They repeatedly claim that victims experience rape as a physical assault like any other. For example, they write:

> To her, the fact that this assault was directed against her sexual organs is—at least at the time—irrelevant. Rape is a physical attack on her person, and she believes she has the right to be protected from such attacks. (1977: 167)

They also claim that women do not regard their sexual organs as "different" from their heads, eyes, or limbs (1977: 167).[4]

Ultimately, the argument that crimes against women are best conceptualized as "violence *not* sex" rests on two premises. The first premise is that the motivation for crimes such as rape and child sexual abuse is not sexual gratification but rather the desire for power, dominance and control, augmented by hostility toward and fear of women in general and the view of women as property. The second premise is that victims experience these crimes as physical assaults. In other words, Clark and Lewis, Brownmiller and the rest claim that sexuality is absent for *both* perpetrators and victims, men and women.

Proponents of the "violence *is* sex" perspective begin with the same observation as their opposites; namely, that socially, wherever sex is present violence is rendered invisible. Carol Smart comments that "violence is not violence if it is sexualized" and that "violence is exonerated if pleasure can be said to be achieved" (1989: 46). But it is not just any pleasure that erases violence: it is the pleasure of those with power. In Catharine MacKinnon's words: "The fact is, anything that anybody with power experiences as sex is considered *ipso facto* not violence, because someone who matters enjoyed it" (1987: 6 n. 19).

If what Smart and MacKinnon describe is in fact a social reality, then it is not surprising that historically the harm of assaults such as rape has gone unrecognized. Accordingly, there appears to be a strategic logic in emphasizing harm, in describing rape as an act of violence, not an act of sex. The drawback to the strategy, write Smart, MacKinnon and others, is that calling something non-sexual does not make it non-sexual. They maintain that the acts themselves, the perceptions of the actors, as well as those of the acted upon all make addressing sex as a constituent factor in rape necessary.

Regarding the acts themselves, Susan Cole offers an interesting consideration. In discussing attempts by feminist activists to have rape legally redefined as assault—a crime of violence, not sex—she notes that the attempts were motivated in part by the awareness that many rapists penetrate victims with objects such as broomsticks rather than with their penises. She goes on:

> That the penis is not a weapon in the assault does not mean that sex is not involved: saying rape is about power and not sex leaves out the crucial fact of where the attackers put their weapons. If rape is about power and not sex, why don't attackers just hit women, and exercise their power that way? Because *rape is sex to them*. (1989: 118)

In other words, it is materially significant that men assault women and girls in their sexual beings, most often directing violence at the parts of their bodies considered to be sexual—breasts and mouths and genitals. The acts themselves, then, are sexual acts, however violent, and that sexual fact cannot be avoided or willed away.

The quote from Cole also refers to the second factor requiring that sex be confronted; namely, the perceptions of the actors. This factor seems to be key. Certainly it is the element most stressed within the "violence *is* sex" perspective. Cole, in refuting the argument that the problem with pornography is the violence alone, points out that "the purpose for all this unspeakable violence was to give a man an erection," and further that "an erection, any way you look at it, is not a fantasy" (1989: 43). In describing serial killers Andrea Dworkin avers:

> They usually mutilate the bodies. Sometimes they have sex before. Sometimes they have sex after. It's all sex to them. Now we can say it's a power trip, but the fact of the matter is that for them, that's the way they have sex. (1991: 40)

Barry similarly claims that "commoditized sex, purchased in prostitution, seized in rape is sex to the aggressor, for whom sexual satisfaction is usually achieved through orgasm" (1985: 172).

MacKinnon, drawing on the recorded comments of perpetrators, gives fullest expression to the argument that the perceptions and experiences of actors encompass sex. Concerning rapists, serial murderers and child molesters she claims:

> [They] enjoy their acts sexually and as men, to be redundant. It is sex *for them*. What is sex except that which is felt as sexual? When acts of dominance and submission, up to and including acts of violence, are experienced as sexually arousing, as sex itself, that is what they are.... Violence is sex when it is practiced as sex. (1987: 6)

This reasoning is conceptually difficult, not least because it appears to suggest an individual subjectivist stance of the sort rejected in my earlier discussion of Kelly's argument on women's self-definition of violence. It also refuses any categorical distinction between violence and sex, and a willingness to criticize the latter as hitherto feminists have criticized the former. This is, of course, precisely MacKinnon's intent. I will explore MacKinnon's critique of sex more fully in a later chapter. Here, the point to be stressed is her claim that perpetrators experience their acts sexually and hence that we cannot neglect the sex in sexual violence.

Some writers further assert that men may experience violence as sex even in the absence of explicit sexual content. Caputi, for example, writes of the sexual significance of violence. She cites research that indicates that a significant number of men experience sexual arousal in response to descriptions of a purely violent event involving a man physically assaulting a woman. Caputi calls such depictions "gorenography" and explains:

> This equation of sex and violence is the essence of gorenography, and I will use the term here to refer to those materials that, although not sexually explicit enough to qualify as pornography (that is, not enough close-up nudity or graphic sexual acts), nonetheless are like pornography ... in that they present violence, domination, torture, and murder in a context that makes these acts sexual. (1992: 210)

Finally, theorists of the "violence *is* sex" perspective contend that victims also perceive what is done to them as sexual. Discussing pornography Cole comments:

> To the women who are in the pictures, it *is* real sex; it happened to them; it is their lives. To the women who are forced by consumers to look at the pornography, or forced to imitate the sex in the pictures, it *becomes* sex in their real lives. (1989: 147)

Similarly, MacKinnon relates the story of a rape victim who could no longer have sex with her husband—a not uncommon experience. Being touched caused her to relive the rape experience, so much so that she would see her husband's face change into the face of the man who raped her. MacKinnon comments: "That, to me, is sexual. When a woman has been raped, and it is sex that she then cannot experience without connecting it to that, it was her sexuality that was violated" (1987: 88).

How are we to assess these contending views? They each draw on the same evidentiary sources to reach opposite conclusions. Clark and Lewis claim rape is like any other assault; Cole claims that where on her body a woman is attacked makes an important difference. Klein states rape is not erotic; Smart states you cannot take the sex out of a sexual act. Herman argues perpetrators are not motivated by the desire for sexual pleasure; Barry argues they are. Clark and Lewis contend that for victims the fact that the assaults were directed at their sexual organs is irrelevant; MacKinnon contends it is central and has a profound, long-lasting effect.

The strength of the "violence *not* sex" account, it seems to me, is its recognition of the role played by power, dominance and control in men's violence against women. In fact, as MacKinnon points out, sexuality itself may be a power structure (1987: 89). If we take the view that sexuality and sexual desire are not "an untainted urge, product of nature" (Hollway 1981: 37), but rather are socially constructed in a culture organized by gender hierarchy, then sexuality as power begins to make sense. In other words, we cannot insulate sexuality from other social relations, including most importantly learned gender roles. Accordingly, sexuality itself is no less gendered than other aspects of social and ontological life. It is gendered such that male sexuality is learned and experienced as domination and female sexuality is learned and experienced as submission. Male sexuality means power; female sexuality means powerlessness.

If male sexuality is a form of power, then it also makes sense that the exercise of power—including violence as one manifestation—may be experienced as sexual, at least for some men. This would account for the research Caputi cites regarding men's sexual arousal in response to descriptions of a purely violent incident. That the incident involved a male assailant and female victim strongly suggests that power is experienced sexually, so that any case of gendered violence at least potentially contains a sexual component for participants and observers alike.

In a similar vein, the hostility and fear Klein, Herman and Brownmiller identify as motives for violence may also be understood to contain a sexual component. The fact that such hatred and fear are expressed so often through *sexual* violence cannot be simply coincidental. Consider the popular belief that rape is the "worst thing" that can happen to a woman. Leaving aside both the accuracy and origin of this belief, one can imagine that a man, driven by hatred and fear, may wish to direct his violence where he believes it will have greatest effect—to strike at his victim's point of greatest vulnerability. Consider further what it is about women these men most hate and fear. Here Wendy Hollway's comments on Peter Sutcliffe (the so-called Yorkshire Ripper) are instructive:

> Sutcliffe hated women for their sexuality, which he split off into prostitutes rather than acknowledge in his wife. Yet he was also obsessed with them. For it is against women's sexuality that men are motivated to measure their masculinity and because they must prove this at each encounter, their masculinity never rests assured. Sutcliffe's desire for "sexual revenge" was not satisfied by one murder. (1981: 39)

The above reflections suggest that the "violence *is* sex" analysis may be seen as an outgrowth of "violence *not* sex" rather than its binary opposite. This challenges us to think beyond static and mutually exclusive categories of violence and sex, to begin to comprehend the extent to which in our society sexuality is gendered and gender is sexualized. From these it is a short step to the eroticization of dominance and submission, including the eroticization of violence. In sum, the "violence is sex" argument requires us to confront simultaneously both the power of sexuality and the sexuality of power.

CONCLUSION

To summarize this chapter, in defining violence against women we need to be cognizant of a number of constitutive elements, some of which remain contested in their specific content among feminist theorists. What follows is a recapitulation, in the form of six statements, of the conclusions I have drawn.

First, so-called personal violence is fundamentally gendered. This means that it is appropriate to identify the subject as men's violence against women. Second, whether we treat men's violence against women as a singular or multiform phenomenon largely depends on context. This means that when we want to draw attention to commonalities among forms of men's violence we speak of "violence," whereas when we want to explore specificities of a discrete, particular form we may see violence as just one manifestation of a range of abusive behaviours. Third and similarly, the term "violence" may denote a general category or a specific action, again depending upon context. Fourth, definitions of violence should be grounded in women's experiences rather than men's perceptions and are best arrived at through a process of collective subjectivity that involves analysis and critique. Fifth, the violence feminists are most concerned with is sex violence, directed at women and girls because they are female and therefore socially deemed vulnerable and subordinate. Finally, the sexual component of men's violence against women cannot be overlooked.

Of these elements, the first, fifth and sixth are pivotal. Together, they epitomize a uniquely feminist understanding of violence, one which stands opposed to received juridical, social, scientific and popular understandings. In Johnson's sense, they "tell the truth." Accordingly, henceforth in this book the subject of violence against women shall be designated *men's sex/ sexual violence.*

As analytical constructs, definitions emerge out of larger attempts to produce theory. They are, in a sense, the "what." The next chapter will address the "why"; that is, feminist discourses on the origins or causes of men's sex/sexual violence.

Notes

1. Implicit in the instrumentalist conception of violence is intentionality. This means that, if the effect of a behaviour is to frighten or coerce the recipient, then frightening or coercing was the actor's intent or purpose.

2. Most of the writers considered in this review focus exclusively on men's violence against women and girls and are silent on the abuse of boys at men's hands. While the incidence of boys suffering abuse is statistically significantly less than that of girls, it is important that we do not forget the boys' experience. To some extent, we can say that boys who are abused by men—especially sexually abused—are feminized, that is, treated as female: not having a self, treated as a sex object, etc.

3. False consciousness is a term usually associated with traditional Marxism. The claim is that the views of oppressed peoples are not legitimate or self-reflexive, but rather are conditioned responses to oppression. When applied to feminism, the false consciousness argument asserts that "while feminist discourse is based on the experiences of women, some women do not rightly know what their experience has been" (Ferguson 1984: 176). What I call epistemic liberalism is the claim that whatever an individual woman says of her experience is true for her. It avoids the discomfort of judgement, but at the cost of making generalization—and hence politics—impossible.

4. Inasmuch as the work of Clark and Lewis derives from a statistical analysis of police reports, rather than first person accounts, one may question the methodological basis for these claims.

2. ORIGINS OF MEN'S SEX/SEXUAL VIOLENCE

Estimates of the incidence of women's victimization are staggering. Citing a variety of sources, MacKinnon states that in the United States, 44 percent of women have experienced rape or attempted rape, including rape in marriage; 43 percent of girls under the age of eighteen have been sexually abused within or outside the family; 85 percent of working women have been sexually harassed at least once in their careers; between 25 percent and 33 percent of women have been battered by their male partners; and about 12 percent of American women are or have been involved in prostitution (1987: 51–52).

While these numbers provide a grim picture of the lives of women, they do not directly tell us much about men; in particular, about the incidence of abusive behaviour among men. For example, if 44 percent of American women have been subjected to rape or attempted rape, we cannot automatically assume that an equivalent 44 percent of American men have raped or attempted to rape. Nor do incarceration statistics tell us much. Some forms of male sex/sexual violence, such as the production and consumption of adult pornography, are not criminalized in most jurisdictions. Forms of sex/sexual violence that are criminalized, such as wife-battering, continue to be under-reported, under-investigated, under-prosecuted and under-punished. Furthermore, the few studies which attempt to measure self-reported anti-woman violence cannot be relied upon, for many men forget or discount their violent behaviour, or they do not recognize it as violence (Hearn 1998).

Since large numbers of women are sexually assaulted by men, this form of violence is practised by a substantial percentage of men. It then becomes difficult to sustain a belief that such behaviour is aberrant. Instead, it begins to look normal, if not normative.[1] And if it is normal, then in seeking explanations for such behaviour we need to look beyond both psychiatry ("These men are sick") and theology ("These men are evil"). Put otherwise, behaviours which are normal, common or typical have their origins in what is shared rather than in what is distinctive. For feminists, this recognition has led to examinations of culture and more particularly of social structure to explain men's sex/sexual violence.[2]

A central explanatory concept for feminist theorists of men's violence is patriarchy. Etymologically, patriarchy refers to a system of rule by older men in their position as heads of households.[3] Many sociologists retain this original meaning of the word, identifying a key issue as the domination of younger men by older men. As a political system, patriarchy so understood leads to curiosities such as one exposed in the United States during the Vietnam War; namely, that men of eighteen were considered old enough to kill and die for their country but not old enough to vote or run for office.

A few feminists coming out of the socialist tradition, such as Heidi Hartmann, retain this generational element in their definition of patriarchy. Most, though, focus exclusively on relations between men and women rather than among men. Accordingly, they use the term patriarchy to mean andarchy—the rule of men. Barry, for example, defines patriarchy as "rule by male right" (1979: 194). Similarly, Sylvia Walby describes patriarchy as "a system of social structures and practices in which men dominate, oppress, and exploit women" (1989: 214). Other feminists eschew the term patriarchy, preferring instead to speak of male supremacy or sometimes male domination. The terms all refer to the same social phenomenon: a consistent pattern of ideological and structural practices which serve to justify and perpetuate men's oppression of women.

The relationship of ideological and structural practices is summarized by Dobash and Dobash in the following quotation:

> The patriarchy is composed of two elements: its structure and its ideology. The structural aspect of the patriarchy is manifest in the hierarchical organization of social institutions and social relations.... It is this institutionalized nature of the hierarchical structure that predetermines which individuals or group will prevail and which ones will be subservient.... The maintenance of such a hierarchical order and the continuation of the authority and advantage of the few is to some extent dependent upon its "acceptance" by the many. It is the patriarchal ideology that serves to reinforce this acceptance. The ideology is supportive of the principle of a hierarchical order, as opposed to an egalitarian one, and of the hierarchy currently in power. It is a rationalization for inequality and serves as a means of creating acceptance of subordination by those destined to such positions. (1979: 43–44)

All systems of hierarchy rest on a principle of difference and the social meanings attached thereto. Legitimizing hierarchy requires that difference be reified and naturalized. Patricia Hill Collins describes this ideological operation in terms of biological determinism. As she says, "At the heart of both racism and sexism are notions of biological determinism claiming that people of African descent and women possess immutable biological characteristics marking their inferiority to elite white men" (1993: 92). Such reification is necessary both to mask the social origins of hierarchy and to maintain an appearance of immutability. For feminist theorists, then, a primary task has been to expose the social construction of gender as difference and to trace the paths by which such construction leads to male sex/sexual violence.

In describing a Marxist approach to ideology, Roger Scruton avers that the principal functions of ideology are "to legitimate, to mystify, and to console" the subordinate class (1983: 213). These functions are accomplished in part through the control of institutions (the education system, organized religion, the family, etc.), which order and sanction social relations so as to constitute and reinforce patterns of dominance whilst also acting as sites and deliverers of ideology. Crucially, as shall be discussed below, it is not enough that men subscribe to this ideology; women must believe it too.

The content of patriarchal or male supremacist ideology is explicated by Dworkin in *Pornography: Men Possessing Women* (1981). She identifies seven "tenets" which justify and legitimate the material realities of male power:

> The power of men is first a metaphysical assertion of self, a *I am* that exists a priori, bedrock, absolute, no embellishment or apology required, indifferent to denial or challenge.... The first tenet of male supremacist ideology is that men have this self and that women must, by definition, lack it.
>
> Second, power is physical strength used over and against others less strong or without the sanction to use strength as power.... The right to physical strength as power, in a male supremacist system, is vouchsafed to men. The second tenet of male supremacy is that men are physically stronger than women and, for that reason, have dominion over them.
>
> Third, power is the capacity to terrorize, to use self and strength to inculcate fear, fear *in* a whole class of persons *of* a whole class of persons.... The third tenet of male supremacist ideology ... is that men are biologically aggressive, inherently combative, eternally antagonistic, genetically cruel, hormonally prone to conflict, irredeemably hostile and warring.
>
> Fourth, men have the power of naming, a great and sublime power. This power of naming enables men to define experience, to articulate boundaries and values, to designate to each thing its realm and qualities, to determine what can and cannot be expressed, to control perception itself.... The fourth tenet of male supremacy is that men, because they are intellectually and creatively existent, name things authentically.
>
> Fifth, men have the power of owning.... The fifth tenet of male supremacy is the presumption that the male's right to own the female and her issue [children and labour] is natural, predating history, postdating progress.
>
> Sixth, the power of money is a distinctly male power.... The sixth tenet of male supremacy is that money properly expresses masculinity.

> Seventh, men have the power of sex.... The seventh tenet of male supremacy is that sexual power authentically originates in the penis. (1981: 13–24)

In this discussion Dworkin demonstrates the relationship between the ideology and the practice of male power. It seems, though, that she has incorporated only half of the ideological equation. As suggested above, the principal targets of ideology are the subordinated. Thus, to take Dworkin's first tenet as an example, while it is important that men believe they have a self and women do not, it is just as important, if not more so, that women believe this. This is the "acceptance" of which Dobash and Dobash speak. To be effective, male supremacist ideology must convince women that men have a self and women do not, that this arrangement is proper or natural, and that cooperating in this arrangement serves the interests of *both* men *and* women.

Male supremacist ideology contributes to the perpetuation of men's sex/sexual violence in two ways. The first is indirect. To take a simple example, ideological assumptions about the public world as male space create ongoing structural discrimination in employment. Many women feel "lucky" to have a job at all and will not risk losing it by complaining of sexual harassment by supervisors, coworkers or customers.[4] Knowing this, some men believe they can harass with impunity. Additionally, the assumption that the public world is or should be an exclusively male preserve creates hostility among men when women attempt to enter.[5] Male supremacist ideology thus contributes to anti-woman violence by creating the material and psychological conditions which make such violence likely.

The second means by which ideology contributes to the perpetuation of male sex/sexual violence is more direct. Sheffield, in discussing "sexual terrorism," describes this link in the following way:

> According to classic theories of political terrorism, an ideology and its spread through propaganda are both necessary *and* sufficient causes of overt violence directed at people who possess a particular ascribed characteristic that legitimates their victimization.... Sexual terrorism, then, is violence perpetuated on girls and women *simply because they are female*, as when the threat of sexual assault keeps many girls and women in a state of fear, regardless of their actual risks. (1987: 175–76)

Sheffield also explains that all forms of terrorism must be justified and that in the case of sexual terrorism, "the ideological underpinnings of patriarchal power relationships serve as ample justification for violence against women" (1987: 172). Thus, under conditions of male supremacy, neither particular provocation nor any other rationalization is necessary to explain and excuse men's sex/sexual violence; the fact of femaleness is provocation enough.

In looking more closely at the operation of ideology, we come to interrelated concepts of oppression, social control, dominance and domination. In the context of these, violence is seen to grow out of male supremacist ideology and simultaneously to enforce that ideology. Collins, for example, maintains that violent acts "are the visible dimensions of a more generalized, routinized system of oppression" (1993: 99). Similarly, Caputi likens femicide to rape in that it is "a social expression of sexual politics, an institutionalized and ritual enactment of domination" (1992: 205). In these examples, violence is portrayed as expressing ideology. It may also, though, realize ideology. Thus, Pauline Bart and Patricia O'Brien argue that "violence and the threat of violence functions as a means of social control, subordinating women" (1985: 1). More broadly, Sheffield claims: "All systems of oppression employ violence or the threat of violence as an institutionalized mechanism for ensuring compliance" (1987: 171).

Brownmiller and Sanday both point to gang rape as the quintessence of violence acting to express and enforce male supremacist ideology. Brownmiller writes:

> No simple conquest of man over woman, group rape is the conquest of men over Woman. It is within the phenomenon of group rape, stripped of the possibility of equal combat, that the male ideology of rape is most strikingly evident. Numerical odds are proof of brutal intention. They are proof too of male bonding ... and proof of a desire to humiliate the victim *beyond* the act of rape through the process of anonymous mass assault. (1975: 187)

In like vein, Sanday describes the motivations for fraternity gang rape:

> Sexual domination is an ever-present theme and concern. Dominance takes a variety of forms—social, sexual, and fraternal. The brothers are concerned to dominate women socially and sexually. Part of the reason they bond as a group is to achieve the domination that they believe is owed to all males. (1990: 124–25)

Inasmuch as men's sex/sexual violence both expresses male power and confirms and consolidates it, the effects of such violence are felt not only by individual victims but by all women in the society. Stanko suggests that consciously or not, all women are aware of their vulnerability. As mentioned in the Introduction, she phrases it, "To walk the streets warily at night is how we actually feel our femininity" (1985: 157). Deborah Cameron and Elizabeth Frazer posit that as much as rape, women fear death at the hands of men, and particularly when a multiple killer is known to be at large, "we often end up living in a state of siege" (1987: 165). Even in absence of a specific threat, awareness of vulnerability governs many women's lives and choices. As Kelly, among others notes: "Whilst not all women live in constant fear, many of women's routine decisions and behaviour are almost automatic measures taken to protect themselves from potential sexual violence" (1988: 32).

Ironically enough, a common strategy among women is to look to individual men for protection. As Hanmer notes: "The pervasive fear of violence, and violence itself, has the effect of driving women to seek protection from men, the very people who commit violence against them" (1978: 229). Radford observes a similar, though more complex pattern:

> The fear of public violence results in the belief that home is the safest place. This discourages women from getting involved in social, political, or even work activities. They become more dependent on individual men for protection from men generally. This dependence on individual men, together with women's resultant isolation, make it easier for those men to assault or abuse the women in the privacy of their own homes. They can do this in the knowledge that it is difficult for women to retaliate or get redress, since such behaviour is supported in the dominant male culture. Legal statements, reproduced in the press, complete the circle by making it clear that men's violence against women is not a concern of the state. (1987: 32)

Another strategy women adopt in the presence of ongoing threat is to deny fear. In Stanko's words, "we feel vulnerable, while at the same time, experience doubt and even denial of our feelings of vulnerability" (1985: 38). In part, denial is a survival technique, a way to live one's life, given that one can neither control one's vulnerability to male sex/sexual violence nor predict when or from where the next attack may come.

Claudia Card, Sheffield, Griffin, Barry, Brownmiller and MacKinnon all depict men's sex/sexual violence as a form of terrorism, exerted upon all women including those who are not direct victims. Barry, for example, writes:

> Sexual violence, by definition, constitutes acts of excess that are unlimited in potential, scope, and depth and that are therefore terrifying to both victims and nonvictims alike. Terrorism goes beyond one woman's experience of sexual violence. It creates a state of existence that captures the hearts and minds of all those who may be potentially touched by it. (1979: 42)

Experience with political terrorism has shown that its strength lies largely in its unpredictability, targeting a whole population but selecting individual victims randomly. One is simply an Israeli on the wrong bus, a Palestinian in the wrong mosque, an Irish Protestant or Catholic in the wrong pub or, as we learned in Oklahoma City, a government employee's child in the wrong daycare at the wrong time. Efforts to avoid terrorist attack come to nothing, precisely because such violence is seemingly random and unpredictable. Of the writers here considered, MacKinnon explores most fully this aspect of the effectiveness of sexual terrorism:

> Sexual abuse works as a form of terror in creating and maintaining this arrangement [of gender inequality]. It is a terror so perfectly motivated and systematically concerted that it never need be intentionally organized.... I have come to think that the unique effectiveness of terrorism ... is that it is at once absolutely systematic and absolutely random: systematic because one group is its target and lives knowing it; random because there is no way of telling who is next on the list. Just to get through another day, women must spend an incredible amount of time, life, and energy cowed, fearful, and colonized, trying to figure out how not to be next on the list.... To be about to be raped is to be gender female in the process of going about life as usual. (1987: 7)

In their concluding essay in an anthology on policing male violence, Hanmer, Radford and Stanko point out that whatever other social roles we may inhabit, we are never free of gender. They write:

> The public and the private, like the division of labour, are converted mentally into materiality where they appear to exist outside and prior to the social relations that make up the orderly patterns of hierarchically structured social life they describe.... The reification of the public and the private is an ideology that explains and justifies the decriminalization of men's violence against women. Viewed on the level of the individual, men and women act in the social world as gendered subjects. This means that not only are the police engaging in a world inhabited by gendered subjects in unequal power relationships, but the police also are gendered and constitute a part of, they are not above or outside, struggles around gendered relations. (1989b: 187)

In western culture under conditions of late capitalism, the content of gender constitutes a series of rigidly enforced binary oppositions, which appear to encourage if not predispose men to be violent toward women. Kelly, for example, writes that as currently constructed in western culture, masculinity "draws on notions of virility, conquest, power, and domination and these themes are reflected in gender relations and heterosexual practice; sex and aggression are linked for most men" (1988: 30–31). Similarly, MacLeod and Saraga assert that "the association of masculinity with domination, of sexual dominance with personal 'success,' is all pervasive" (1988: 41). It follows that if masculinity requires dominance, its binary opposite, femininity, requires submission. Addressing some specific implications of this social construct, Sheffield states:

> Sexual terrorism is maintained by a system of sex-role socialization that encourages men to be terrorists in the name of masculinity and women to be victims in the name of femininity.... To the extent that the essence of femininity is defined as an innate masochism, coerciveness is rationalized away. (1987: 182)

Both Cole and Herman point out that the relationship of constructed gender and experience is two-directional. Just as femininity creates women who can be victimized, so too does victimization create feminine women. Commenting on the psychological effects of child sexual abuse and wife assault, Cole writes:

> Cultural products and socialized sexual roles are not the only things that keep women in line with the prevailing sexual ideology. Real experience works just as well. (1989: 117)

On the experience of incest Herman suggests:

> The similarities between the incest victims and the daughters of seductive fathers once again confirm the contention that incest represents a common pattern of traditional female socialization carried to a pathological extreme. Covert incest fosters the development of women who overvalue men and undervalue women, including themselves. Overt incest fosters the development of women who submit to martyrdom and sexual slavery. (1981: 125)

Finally, on the subject of gender enforcement, Michael S. Kimmel offers this insight:

> The rules of masculinity and femininity are strictly enforced. And difference equals power. The difference between male and female sexuality reproduces men's power over women, and, simultaneously, the power of some men over other men, especially of the dominant, hegemonic forms of manhood—white, straight, middle-class— over marginalized masculinities. Those who dare to cross over ...

risk being seen as *gender*, not sexual nonconformists. (1990: 122–23)

Constructed and enforced gender contributes to sets of understandings about self and other. Within the context of feminist theories on the origins of men's sex/sexual violence, three such sets are particularly relevant: men's understandings of themselves; men's understandings of women; and men's understandings of other men. In discussions of men's understandings of themselves, a single theme emerges: that of right or entitlement. A sense of entitlement is, as Kimmel comments, "offered to boys as part of their birthright" (1990: 127). Men learn to feel entitled to unrestricted sexual access to women, sometimes especially against women's will (Cameron and Frazer 1987: 164); entitled to constant emotional attention (Klein 1981: 75); entitled to goods and services from women as a class (Bart and O'Brien 1985: 100); and entitled to kill when women thwart them (Caputi and Russell 1992: 18). Social supports for men's experience of entitlement go beyond boyhood lessons, encompassing law, "common sense" and cultural beliefs. Herman's comment in relation to child sexual abuse is illustrative:

> It is this attitude of entitlement—to love, to service, and to sex— that finally characterizes the incestuous father and his apologists. In a patriarchal society, the concept of the father's right to use female members of his family—especially his daughters—as he sees fit is implicit even in the structure of the incest taboo. (1981: 49)

Relative degrees of entitlement, however, vary. In the west, hegemonic men—white, middle-class, able-bodied, heterosexual—feel and are encouraged to feel rather greater entitlement than their non-hegemonic brothers. Similarly, entitlement may vary depending upon a man's relationship to a particular woman. The incestuous father Herman describes may feel he has a right to impose sexual demands on his own daughter but not on another man's child. Dobash and Dobash note that a marital relationship gives a man "both the perceived right and the obligation to control his wife's behaviour and thus the means to justify beating her" (1979: 93). Klein calls this entitlement "patriarchal rights of discipline" (1981: 75). And Kelly argues:

> Sexual access, like other resources, is determined by relational power. The more power a man can claim over a particular woman, the greater his claim to exclusive access. The greater his perceived right to exclusive sexual access, the more likely it is that some level of sexual aggression will be considered legitimate. (1988: 30)

In contrast to the single theme of entitlement in discussions of men's understandings of themselves, feminist analysis reveals two distinct motifs in men's gendered view of women. The first of these involves objectification and attitudes of proprietariness. Cole describes objectification as "the process through which the person on the bottom of the hierarchy is dehumanized, made less human than the person on the top of the hierarchy, who in turn becomes the standard for what human is" (1989: 26). But objectification goes beyond depersonalization. It involves the transformation of *somebody* into *something*—"thingification," as MacKinnon puts it (1987: 54). Sometimes these things, these objects are a collection of body parts—"tits, cunt, and ass" is how Russell sums it up (1993a: 6)—which serves men's sexual and reproductive purposes. They are "controllable as objects are controllable" (Dworkin 1981: 65) and just as importantly, as objects they can be "disposed of or replaced" (Radford 1992: 5).

In western culture objects are owned, so it is not surprising that objectification coexists with proprietariness in men's understandings of women. Both Brownmiller and Clark and Lewis note that rape was originally conceived of as a property crime. Dobash and Dobash comment that a husband's sense of ownership and control is immediate upon marrying, for it is embedded in the marriage contract and associated social meanings (1979: 94).[6] And Russell points out that for some men, ownership of wives is not extinguished when the marriage dissolves: "The phenomenon of rape by ex-husbands is another manifestation of the concept of wives as property; even divorce, for some men, does not alter their right to their property" (1982: 237). Perhaps the best summation of men's view of women as property and the social supports for such a view is provided by Margo Wilson and Martin Daly in their article on men who kill their wives (uxoricide):

> Men exhibit a tendency to think of women as sexual and reproductive "property" that they can own and exchange.... Proprietariness implies a more encompassing mind-set, referring not just to the emotional force of one's own feelings of entitlement but to a more pervasive attitude toward social relationships. Proprietary entitlements in people have been conceived and institutionalized as identical to proprietary entitlements in land, chattels, and other economic resources. (1992: 85)

The second motif feminists have identified in men's perceptions of women stands in sharp contrast to the first. Whereas objectification and proprietariness suggest a certain emotional detachment, the second theme is highly charged, its recurring operative terms being hatred, fear, rage and anger. It is misogyny. Some theorists speak of generalized misogyny. Stanko, for example, suggests that serial rapists who attack women unknown to them are acting out of "anger toward women or a hatred of women" (1985: 97). Russell writes that pornography can "undermine male inhibitions against acting out the rage they feel toward women" (1993b: 258). Caputi discusses violence against women as hate crimes as follows:

> The reigning, though denied, mood is *hatred*, sexually political hatred. A "Hate crime" is conventionally defined as "any assault, intimidation, or harassment that is due to the victim's race, religion, or ethnic background." That definition obviously must be expanded to include gender (as well as sexual preference). Vast numbers of women are now suffering and dying from various forms of hate crimes worldwide, including neglect, infanticide, genital mutilation, battering, rape, and murder. What men call "peacetime," researcher Lori Heise truthfully names a "global war on women." (1993: 22)

Other theorists propose a more specific target. It is not simply women *qua* women men hate and fear, they say, but women's sexuality. Thus Barry describes pimping and procuring as "about the most complete expressions of male hatred for femaleness" (1979: 86). Sheffield argues that men perceive female sexuality as a "threatening force" and hence that out of their own fear, have sought to bring this force under control "by both physical and psychological means" (1987: 172). I've already mentioned Hollway's claim that Peter Sutcliffe used prostitutes rather than acknowledge his wife as a sexual being. Cameron and Frazer further posit that as emblems of female sexuality, women involved in prostitution are especially subject to hate-motivated violence. This is because, as they argue:

> The prostitute here functions as an archetype: she represents the sexual aspect of all women. So the ambivalent responses the prostitute calls forth are part of men's feelings about women in general. The desire to kill prostitutes is thus not sharply distinct from sadism: it is another outcome of the same conflation of sex, transgression, hatred, and death. (1987: 131)

The two motifs of objectification and hate brought together in Brownmiller's discussion of the meaning of rape bear repeating:

> Like assault rape is an act of physical damage to another person, and like robbery it is also an act of acquiring property: the intent is to "have" the female body in the acquisitory meaning of the term. A woman is perceived by the rapist both as hated person and desired property. Hostility *against her and possession* of her may be simultaneous motivations, and the hatred for her is expressed in the same act that is the attempt to "take" her against her will. In one

violent crime, rape is an act against person and property. (1975: 185)

The third set of gendered understandings relevant to feminist analyses of the origins of male sex/sexual violence is men's perceptions of other men. Like the previous set, it also contains two distinct themes. The first of these involves identification, bonding and collaboration. Men identify with other men, even—sometimes especially—when those other men are known to be sexually violent toward women. Caputi, among others, states that male identification with the killer is a recurrent pattern in cases of sensationalized sex murder (1993: 15). Hence Jack the Ripper, Peter Sutcliffe and Marc Lépine are lionized in men's songs, poetry and football chants.[7] Two partial explanations for this identification with and celebration of sexist killers and other violent men is provided by Larry May and Robert Strikwerda. In an article on men's collective responsibility for rape they write first that "some men are not unlike the rapist, since they would be rapists if they had the opportunity to be placed into a situation where their inhibitions against rape were removed" (1994: 146). Identification, then, derives in part from a recognition of shared desire and the vicarious pleasure thereof. More fundamentally, though, May and Strikwerda argue that unity among men depends to some degree upon oppression of and violence against women. In their words: "Male bonding is made easier because there is an 'Other' that males can bond 'against.' And this other is the highly sexualized stereotype of the 'female'" (1994: 147).

On the subject of male bonding and its relationship to sex/sexual violence, Sanday's study of fraternity gang rape offers the fullest exploration. Her central thesis is that participation in acts of communal sexual violence is a necessary condition both for the individual's self-identity as a full-fledged man and for group cohesion. She discusses the practice of "pulling train," in which a number of men sexually assault a single, often drugged or otherwise incapacitated woman, in the presence of their fellows. Participation is at once a rite of passage that forever changes the individual's identity and understanding of masculinity; a homoerotic act in which men have sex with each other through the medium of a woman's body; and a bonding ritual, bringing the brothers together as "virile, heterosexual, loyal comrades" (1990: 133). Generalizing beyond the specific case of fraternity gang rape Sanday states:

> Cross-cultural research demonstrates that whenever men build and give allegiance to a mystical, enduring, all-male social group, the disparagement of women is, invariably, an important ingredient of the mystical bond, and sexual aggression the means by which the bond is renewed. As long as exclusive male clubs exist in a society that privileges men as a social category, we must recognize that collective sexual aggression provides a ready stage on which some

men represent their social privilege and introduce adolescent boys
to their future place in the status hierarchy. (1990: 19–20)

Collaboration among men need not involve direct participation in
shared acts of sex/sexual violence. In supporting their claim that men in
western culture are collectively responsible for rape May and Strikwerda
list five points, three of which address non-participatory collaboration:

(2) Insofar as some men, by the way they interact with other
(especially younger) men, contribute to a climate in our society
where rape is made more prevalent, then they are collaborators in
the rape culture and for this reason share in the responsibility for
rapes committed in that culture.

(4) In addition, insofar as many other men could have prevented
fellow men from raping, but did not act to prevent these actual
rapes, then these men also share responsibility along with the
rapists.

(5) Finally, insofar as some men benefit from the existence of rape
in our society, these men also share responsibility along with the
rapists. (1994: 146)

Hollway traces collaborative attitudes among men in elite discourses
on instances of sensationalized sex murder, specifically the case of Peter
Sutcliffe. She states:

Sutcliffe's trial demonstrated men's collaboration with other men
in the oppression of women. As the mouthpieces for legal,
psychiatric, and journalistic discourses, men collaborated in
reproducing a view of the world which masks men's violence against
women.... The trial refused to recognize the way in which Sutcliffe's
acts were an expression—albeit an extreme one—of the construction
of an aggressive masculine sexuality and of women as its objects.
This "cover up" exonerates men in general even when one man is
found guilty. (1981: 33)

And where Hollway sees collaboration in acts of "cover up," Griffin sees it
in "protection rackets." Thus, she argues that "In the system of chivalry,
men protect women against other men.... Indeed, chivalry is an age-old
protection racket which depends for its existence on rape" (1978: 320).
    The second theme emerging out of feminist analyses of men's rela-
tionship with other men cannot be easily reconciled with the first. Identification, bonding and collaboration all bespeak a sense of oneness with

other men, including particularly men known to be violent to women. In contrast, the second theme is characterized by disunity, in that it focuses on fear. Of the writers considered in this review, Kimmel in particular gives expression to this theme. Writing on well-publicized cases of sex/sexual violence and their relationship to ordinary American men he asks:

> What is it about groups that seems to bring out the worst in men? I think it is because the animating condition for most American men is a deeply rooted fear of other men—a fear that other men will view us as less than manly. The fear of humiliation, of losing in a competitive ranking among men, of being dominated by other men—these are the fears that keep men in tow and that reinforce traditional definitions of masculinity as a false definition of safety. (1990: 127)

Michael Kaufman links men's fear of other men to early experiences of male violence. He writes:

> [T]hese early experiences of violence caused an incredible amount of anxiety and required a huge expenditure of energy to resolve. That anxiety is crystallized in an unspoken fear (particularly among heterosexual men): all other men are my potential humiliators, my enemies, my competitors. (1997: 42)

Dworkin (1981) further suggests that men learn to fear male violence and that, paradoxically, such fear forms the basis of men's commitment to violence. According to Dworkin,

> Men develop a strong loyalty to violence. Men must come to terms with violence because it is the prime component of male identity. Institutionalized in sports, the military, acculturated sexuality, the history and mythology of heroism, it is taught to boys until they have become its advocates—men, not women. Men become advocates of that which they most fear. In advocacy they experience mastery of fear. In mastery of fear they experience freedom. (1981: 51)

The transformation of fear of men and associated anger toward men into violence against women is also postulated by MacLeod and Saraga in their critique of theories of child sexual abuse. They suggest that:

> instead of seeing the source of sexual violence in rage at the mother, perhaps it should be seen as rage at men, at the father, at the self, that is displaced onto and acted out against women and children,

and instead of perceiving other men as threatening, which is terrifying and unacceptable, the threat is perceived in women where it can be controlled. (1988: 42)

These three sets of understandings, and the construct of gender from which they derive, distill into one key social fact: men are people who do violence and women are people who suffer it. In part this means that women constitute socially sanctioned appropriate targets for male violence. It is not enough, then, to simply say men learn to be violent; men learn to *direct* violence at women and children. As Klein writes, "the crucial point is not that men are frustrated and take it out on the next person. It is that men are structurally and psychologically accustomed to taking it out on women" (1981: 72).

Some feminists go further, claiming that for some men anyway, masculine identity requires evidence in the form of hurt or dead women. Thus Cameron and Frazer, in discussing the function of flashing and rape, state: "Both are acts which men do in order to reassure themselves of their power and potency; both include, as a crucial factor in that reassurance, the fear and humiliation of the female victims" (1987: 164). Hollway, too, claims men must constantly prove their masculinity on the bodies of women. This need for constant reassurance meant, in the case of Peter Sutcliffe, that his "desire for 'sexual revenge' was not satisfied by one murder" (1981: 39).

As argued earlier, the content of gender in western culture equates masculinity with dominance and femininity with submission. Hence gendered sexuality—desire, pleasure, expression—is constructed to conform to this pattern. MacKinnon explains that as long as gender inequality persists, society will be divided into two communities of interest:

> The male [community of interests] centrally features hierarchy of control. Aggression against those with less power is experienced as sexual pleasure, an entitlement of masculinity. For the female, subordination is sexualized, in the way that dominance is for the male, as pleasure as well as gender identity, as femininity. Dominance, principally by men, and submission, principally by women, will be the ruling code through which sexual pleasure is experienced. Sexism will be a political inequality that is sexually enjoyed, if unequally so. (1987: 6–7)

The process of constructing gendered sexualities that MacKinnon describes is often referred to as the "eroticization of dominance and submission." This term encapsulates two mutually reinforcing thought constructs relating to male sexuality. The first is that "real sex" requires dominance, aggression, conquest, violation. The "best sex" for some men, then, is that which involves the least consent or mutuality. Russell, in her work on wife rape, describes strategies for achieving non-consensual sex:

> A man can only rape an uncooperative woman. Men whose wives always submit to them have to look elsewhere if they want non-consenting sex. And of course many married rapists do just that: they rape women other than their wives. Others create a non-consenting situation in their marriages by beating up their wives and then having sex with them. (1982: 132)

Barry similarly suggests that the desire for non-mutual sex is common to both men who use prostitutes and men who rape. As she argues:

> For customers [of prostitutes] this [the sexual encounter, particularly the act of fellatio] constitutes an essentially non-interactive, non-mutual sexual experience which establishes the basis for further demands of perversions and violence in the exchange. This is the same sex which is seized and forced in rape and other forms of sexual violence.... It is from this analysis of the interaction of prostitution through its sexual commoditization and rape that the etiology of crimes against women is traced back to the social construction of a deviant male sexuality which appears to be the same for the customers of prostitutes and for rapists. (1985: 172)

Interestingly enough, both Russell and Sanday quote informants who attribute the appeal for some men of the sexual practice of fellatio to its non-mutuality. Here is Russell's Mrs. Eriksen:

> He felt fellatio was a means by which a woman is made subservient to a man. He enjoyed the gesture: that I was bowing my head to his penis. It was the subservient posture that he wanted as much as the physical pleasure he derived from it. (1982: 124)

Mrs. Eriksen's understanding is supported by an exchange between a male interviewer and a fraternity member included in Sanday's study:

> There are many reasons why oral sex is so gratifying. A blowjob is significant because the emphasis is so completely on having the woman devote herself to our pleasure. In other words, it is the least mutual form of love-making. In posture, sensation, and emotional content, a blowjob involves the most subservience to the man's desires. (1990: 123)

The idea that "real sex" requires dominance is reciprocated by one in which dominance is experienced as sexy. As described in the first chapter, Caputi cites research indicating that depictions of gendered violence, devoid of explicit sexual content, provoke arousal in a significant portion of men. Similarly, in a discussion of wife-battering, MacKinnon argues that all gendered violence has a sexual component:

> But when violence against women is eroticized as it is in this culture, it is very difficult to say that there is a major distinction in the level of sex involved between being assaulted by a penis and being assaulted by a fist, especially when the perpetrator is a man. If women as gender female are defined as sexual beings, and violence is eroticized, then men violating women has a sexual component. (1987: 92)

I will return to this quotation in the context of MacKinnon's broader critique of sex. Here the point to be stressed is her contention that where violence, as a manifestation of dominance, is eroticized, the experience of violence is at least partially a sexual experience. This brings to mind Russell's comments about men seeking non-consensual sex. One scenario she runs is men beating their wives in order to create conditions in which consent is unlikely. While that may sometimes be the case, the analyses by Caputi and MacKinnon suggest an alternative interpretation: sometimes, men find the act of beating their wives arousing, which then leads them to want/demand sexual intercourse. Both these scripts originate in the eroticization of dominance and submission. The first illustrates some men's wish to express dominance when they are being sexual; the second their wish to express sexuality when they are being dominant. The question remains, where does the eroticization of dominance and submission itself come from?

What is taken to be erotic is learned as a constituent of gendered sexuality. Like all learning, it is a social/cultural process in which individuals are taught both desire and meaning by the culture in which they live. Cameron and Frazer describe this process in terms of prevailing cultural representations:

> Representations will construct and shape peoples' desires by offering them certain objects, certain channels, certain meanings. What aspirations and pleasures are available, what practices, identities, and dreams are even thinkable is determined to a very large extent by the culture. Our culture has violent, pornographic dreams; it has aspirations to (male) freedom and transcendence. Not coincidentally, it has sadistic sexual murder. (1987: 142–43)

The "violent, pornographic dreams" of western culture are manufactured, in the literal sense, in the multibillion dollar industry of pornography. As representation[8] and as practice, the pornography industry is deeply implicated in the cultural eroticization of dominance and submission and is rightly subject to extensive feminist criticism. John Stoltenberg, for example, avers that domination and subordination have become so culturally eroticized as to be almost physically addictive. He goes on to argue:

> Pornography also *eroticizes* male supremacy. It makes dominance and subordination feel like sex; it makes hierarchy feel like sex; it makes force and violence feel like sex; it makes hate and terrorism feel like sex; it makes inequality feel like sex. Pornography keeps sexism sexy. It keeps sexism *necessary* for some people to have sexual feelings. (1993: 69)

I define pornography as a practice which eroticizes dominance and submission in words, pictures and live display. The purpose of pornography is to give its consumers sexual excitement including but not limited to erection and ejaculation. As revealed by Linda Marchiano (1981) and Elly Danica (1988), in both commercial and home-grown settings women and children are harmed in the production of pornography—physically intimidated, beaten, raped, threatened with weapons, drugged. Other women and children are harmed by being forced to replicate the postures of submission found in pornographic magazines and videos. Still other women and children are harmed by rapists and other men who consume pornography prior to attacking their victims. Finally, women and children are harmed when pornography is put on public display such as to make the school, workplace, shop or larger environment a more dangerous and alienated place for women and children.[9]

Pornography is a powerful agent in the cultural eroticization of violence against women not just because of its pervasiveness,[10] but also because of the way it links public representation and private experience. In her introduction to an anthology of feminist analyses of pornography, Russell states that much of pornography is designed as a masturbation tool for men. She explains:

> Because the pleasure of ejaculation becomes associated with degrading depictions of women, the sexual pleasure serves as a particularly powerful reinforcer for the masturbator, who learns to be turned on by the degradation itself. Because men's viewing of pornography frequently culminates in orgasm, the lessons of pornography are learned much faster and more tenaciously than when they view nonpornographic media. They also develop a strong stake in keeping it at their disposal. (1993a: 17–18)

Cole similarly contends that the values espoused in pornography are learned "not just in our heads, but in our bodies" (1989: 51). She goes on to suggest:

> Because we experience sex in our bodies, it is tempting to believe that whatever our bodies do is natural. But therein lies the overwhelming power of sexual ideology: it does not work on the level of ideas, it works right in our bodies, making it seem not like a constructed set of social values, but like another natural fact of life. (1989: 127)

SUMMARY

This chapter began with a discussion of the normalcy of men's sex/sexual violence. That is the starting place of all feminist analyses: that men's threatening, intimidating, abusive and violent behaviours are not aberrant and hence have their origins in commonalities of culture and social structure. I then went on to explore feminist discourses on ideological and structural practices of what is variously called patriarchy, andarchy, male supremacy and male domination. I considered how such practices contribute to the perpetuation of men's sex/sexual violence and to the ideological functions of oppression, social control and dominance. These led to an examination of the effects of men's sex/sexual violence on all women in a society and common feminist characterizations of men's violence as a form of terrorism.

Next, gender analysis was applied to sexuality. In this, particular attention was paid to the relationship of gendered sexuality to violence. What is called the eroticization of dominance and submission was explored in terms of two corresponding notions relating to male sexuality: sex requires dominance and dominance is experienced as sexual. Feminist hypotheses on how dominance and submission come to be eroticized were briefly explored.

Having considered the relationship of sex and violence, I turn now to the critique of sex and sexuality themselves. For this MacKinnon is the leading guide.

NOTES

1. For two very different treatments of the normalness of male violence see Theweleit 1987 and Bourke 1999.
2. One alternative is to seek biological explanations. The field of sociobiology has been extensively critiqued by feminists and others as both methodologically unsound and ideologically driven. See for example works by Ruth Hubbard and Marion Lowe.
3. The Greek root *pater* is variously translated as head of household, father and owner of slaves.
4. Stanko, however, notes that highly educated women report more workplace

harassment and that this may be because "their presence in non-traditional jobs [is] more threatening to their male peers" (1985: 62).

5. Of course, the public world is full of women: secretaries, waitresses, etc. The issue really is which roles are filled by women and men respectively.

6. This may be less true today than it was when the Dobashs wrote it in 1979, as increasingly couples are defining their own perimeters to their marriage contract.

7. In the weeks following the Montreal massacre, fraternity houses at several Canadian universities hung banners declaring "Marc was right." In December 1992, the third anniversary of the massacre, a community newspaper in Vancouver, British Columbia, published a poem praising Lépine's actions and saying he did not go far enough. Members of the disgraced and now disbanded Canadian Airborne Regiment held a Marc Lépine Memorial Celebration party on the anniversary prior to their notorious Somalia mission. On the celebration of Jack the Ripper, Ted Bundy and other sex criminals, see Caputi 1993: 13–15. On the footballs chants for Peter Sutcliffe, see Cameron and Frazer 1987: 165.

8. There is some debate among feminists as to whether pornography should be described as representation. Collins and Longino both use the term, but MacKinnon and Cole both object to it. Their point is that pornography is more than words and pictures, it is a "sexual reality" (MacKinnon 1987: 173) in which sexual events are documented (Cole 1989: 27). I use the term in the sense of broadcasted description and characterization.

9. Other definitions of pornography exist and, in particular, there is a growing debate within feminism about the possibilities of woman-positive, woman-controlled pornography. This debate is not the subject of this chapter, but I refer readers to Druscilla Cornell's anthology *Feminism and Pornography* (2000) for a variety of different perspectives on these debates.

10. A number of feminist writers, including MacKinnon, have noted that in the United States there are more pornography outlets than McDonald's restaurants.

3. MacKinnon on Sex and Sexuality

The discussion in the previous chapter on the origins of men's sex/sexual violence leads to Catherine MacKinnon's critique of sex and sexuality.[1] Her argument is complex but nevertheless is foundational to a growing body of feminist theory enunciated by a number of writers. At the same time, the critique is not without controversy.

MacKinnon's starting place is an argument for the centrality of sexuality in feminist theory and in life. Her well-known analogy is to Marxism: "Sexuality is to feminism what work is to Marxism" (1987: 48).[2] Just as Marxism takes work (relations of production) as its chief focus and the fundamental axis around which social relations are organized, so feminism views sexuality (relations of re-production) as its chief focus and society's basic organizing principle. In MacKinnon's words:

> By saying that sexuality is to feminism what work is to Marxism, I mean that both sexuality and work focus on that which is most one's own, that which most makes one the being the theory addresses, as that which is most taken away by what the theory criticizes. (1987: 48)

Sexuality, then, is not simply one more arena in which gendered relations of male dominance and female submission are played out; rather, sexuality is foundational to gender. According to MacKinnon, "The moulding, direction, and expression of sexuality organize society into two sexes, women and men. This division underlies the totality of social relations" (1987: 49). Sexuality is "a pervasive dimension of social life, one that permeates the whole, a dimension along which gender occurs and through which gender is socially constituted" (1989: 130). In short, sexuality is "definitive" in the process of the subordination of women to men (1989: 128).

MacKinnon looks at the content of sexuality and the content of gender and finds them to be identical. She writes:

> If gender is a social construct, and sexuality is a social construct, and the question is, of what is each constructed, the fact that their contents are identical—not to mention that the word sex refers to both—might be more than a coincidence. (1989:143)

Sexuality and gender then become "functions" of each other (1989: 143), such that "sexuality is gendered as gender is sexualized" (1987: 50). Gender and sexuality are different expressions of an underlying social equation of

Figure 1: Cycle of Male Sexual Desire

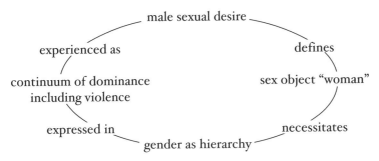

the male with dominance and the female with submission. Enjoying the equation as erotic is the domain of sexuality (1989: 143). Identity, an erected role defined as the self, is the domain of gender. To be gender female is to be passive, subservient and at all times sexually available to men either directly or through the medium of pornography. These terms also define female sexuality. Gender makes hierarchy sexy while sexuality makes gender hierarchical. Within these, violence is pivotal.

According to MacKinnon, male sexual desire creates or defines the sexual object "woman" which necessitates gender as hierarchy which in turn is expressed in violence such that violence is experienced as sexual. This cyclical process may be pictured as in Figure 1.

In her extensive writings on pornography MacKinnon often describes it as *revealing* male sexuality; she does at points suggest that pornography also *configures* male sexuality in particular ways. She writes, for example, that pornography "conditions male orgasm to female subordination. It tells men what sex means, what a real woman is, and codes them together in a way that is behaviourally reinforcing" (1987: 190). More broadly, MacKinnon repeatedly stresses that sexuality is always fundamentally social. In *Feminism Unmodified* she defines sexuality as "whatever a given society eroticizes. That is, sexual is whatever sexual means in a particular society" (1987: 53). She expands on this analysis in *Toward a Feminist Theory of the State*. She argues the following:

> The general theory of sexuality emerging from this feminist critique does not consider sexuality to be an inborn force inherent in individuals, nor cultural in the Freudian sense, in which sexuality exists in a cultural context but in universally invariant stages and psychic representations. It appears instead to be culturally specific, even if so far largely invariant because male supremacy is largely universal, if always in specific forms. Although some of its abuses (like prostitution) are accentuated by poverty, it does not vary by class, although class is one hierarchy it sexualizes. Sexuality be-

comes, in this view, social and relational, constructing and constructed of power. (1989: 151)

This last is key: that male sexuality simultaneously constructs power and is
itself constructed of power. The wish to define a sexual object according
to one's requirements for arousal and satisfaction remains only a wish,
unless one has the power to impose that definition. The need for hierarchy
in male sexual experience remains unfulfilled unless hierarchy can be
enforced. And so on. In short, the sexuality/gender cycle modelled above
only makes sense if we situate it as *embedded in a substratum of male supremacy*,
as depicted in Figure 2. That substratum in turn is nurtured and reinforced
by the power generated in and through the sexuality/gender cycle. As
MacKinnon, in a rather different context, sums up: "I think that men are
the way they are because they have power, more than that they have power
because they are the way they are" (1987: 220). In other words, there is
nothing *inherently* masculine about the exercise of power. Rather, under
conditions of male supremacy power defines the masculine.

In her extensive critique of sex and sexuality, MacKinnon pays scant
attention to the experiences and meanings of lesbianism and homosexuality. In both *Feminism Unmodified* and *Toward a Feminist Theory of the State*
there are only a few scattered references and no sustained analysis. As I see
it, she subsumes lesbianism into homosexuality and subsumes homosexuality into heterosexuality. She writes, for example, that lesbian sex "does
not by definition transcend the eroticization of dominance and submission
and their social equation with masculinity and femininity" (1989: 119). She
locates lesbian and gay sexuality within the gendered sexual system. Of gay
men MacKinnon avers that to the extent that they "choose men because
they are men, the meaning of masculinity is affirmed as well as undermined"
(1989: 142). Finally, she summarizes: "It may also be that sexuality is so
gender marked that it carries dominance and submission with it, whatever
the gender of its participants" (1989: 142).

Figure 2: Male Supremacy and Cycle of Male Sexual Desire

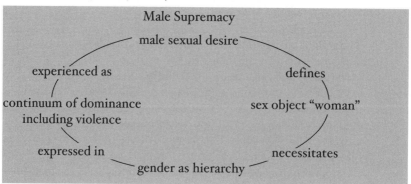

It would appear that MacKinnon conceives of only one model of lesbian relationships, that of butch/femme or sadomasochism's top and bottom. She fails to acknowledge the possibility of mutuality between lesbian partners, a pattern of relationship that I would claim is at least as prevalent as the hierarchy of butch/femme. And while it is true some gay men display a kind of hyper-masculinity, and attendant misogyny, this is not always the case.

In her most recent work (2003) MacKinnon ponders whether for lesbians gender precedes sexuality. She approvingly quotes Charles Silverstein, who claims that "lesbians are first and foremost women and only secondarily gay" (quoted at 2003c: 1160). Yet like gay men, lesbians are "traitors" to their gender. MacKinnon continues: "The demand for gender loyalty is, in turn, an essential precondition to the enforcement of patriarchy. Thus, the oppression of gay men and lesbians is linked to the oppression of women as women, either heterosexual or lesbian" (2003c: 1161). MacKinnon goes on to cite Andrew Koppelman describing lesbianism as a form of "insubordination" (2003c: 1176) to the extent that it denies that female sexuality exists solely for the sake of male gratification. MacKinnon concludes this work with an argument that same-sex discrimination is sex discrimination based on four premises: 1) that sexuality is a social construct of gender; 2) that sexuality partly defines gender inequality in unequal societies; 3) that same-sexuality challenges the sex roles of gender inequality; and 4) that sexual orientation discrimination is sex discrimination (2003c: 1183–86). Finally, in the closing sentence of the book, MacKinnon refers to the "transformative potential of gay and lesbian liberation" (2003c: 1190) but leaves that potential unexplored.

PORNOGRAPHY

MacKinnon is probably best known for her work on pornography. The anti-pornography "model ordinance" developed by MacKinnon and Andrea Dworkin will be discussed in Chapter VII. Here I will address her underlying critique of pornography and, in turn, Judith Butler's critique of that analysis.

It is crucial to understand that in MacKinnon's view, pornography is more than words and pictures. Rather, pornography is a political practice, one which conditions male sexual gratification to the violation and degradation of women. Commenting on a homemade videotape of a rape she writes: "For the viewer who takes pleasure in her pain, however, the distinction between pain and pleasure does not exist. Her pain is his pleasure" (1993b: 114 n. 4). This applies to the women and children who are used in the production of pornography and the women and children upon whom pornography is used.

Pornography works, according to MacKinnon, because it transmogrifies abuse into sex for men. As she states:

> In pornography, there it is, in one place ... all the *unspeakable* abuse: the rape, the battery, the sexual harassment, the prostitution, and the sexual abuse of children. Only in pornography it is called something else: sex, sex, sex, sex, and sex respectively. Pornography sexualizes rape, battery, sexual harassment, prostitution, and child sexual abuse; it thereby celebrates, promotes, authorizes, and legitimizes them. More generally, it eroticizes the dominance and submission that is the dynamic common to them all. It makes hierarchy sexy and calls that "the truth about sex" [Foucault] or just a mirror of reality. Through this process pornography constructs what a woman is as what men want from sex. This is what pornography means. (1987: 171)

If we deconstruct this quotation, we come to a series of understandings. The first is that the acts enumerated are unspeakable, having, in other words, no place in public discourse, at least until feminists came to name them. The second is that pornography sexualizes the unspeakable and in so doing, advocates them, makes them desirable for men. Third, in advocating violence against women, pornography eroticizes the underlying dynamic of dominance and submission. Fourth, that dynamic is normalized and in so doing defines what a woman is. To this last I would add that it also defines what a man is. In particular, pornography juxtaposes the man as not woman, not exploited, not used, not powerless.

In the United States, those who oppose the regulation of pornography argue that as expression, pornography is protected by the First Amendment to the U.S. Constitution, which guarantees free speech. MacKinnon responds that the content of the pornographer's speech is a woman's life: "This is women's version of life imitating art: our life as the pornographer's text" (1993b: 7). Centrally, the pornographer's text is "a form of forced sex, a practice of sexual politics, an institution of gender inequality" (1989: 197). To those who claim that pornography is representation she responds: "If, by contrast, representation *is* reality ... then pornography is no less an act than the rape and torture it represents" (1993b: 29). It is not just that women and children are harmed in the production of pornography, though that is true, but that all women and children are targeted through pornography. Courts have recognized, though not expressly stated, that "group-based attacks are directed at every individual group member within range" (1993b: 52).

Some commentators express concern that in arguing against the view that pornography is representation, MacKinnon misses a point. As Karen Boyle argues:

> to see pornographic films or photographs as a documentary record of abuse distorts the fact that they are also fictionalised represen-

tations. As anti-pornography feminists argue that the pleasure in pornographic texts cannot simply be read as "real" pleasure, so it is important to remember that their representations of rape cannot be assumed to be "real" rape. Anti-pornography feminists are—often justifiably—criticised for reading evidence of abuse from pornographic images, assuming an uncomplicated relationship between representation and reality. (Dworkin's ground breaking work *Pornography* (1981) is particularly guilty of this.) While it is not always possible to distinguish between representation and abuse (e.g., in the filming of war rape), it is a mistake to collapse the one into the other (i.e., to argue that a pornographic rape scenario is always and necessarily the rape of the performer). Such a strategy can be extremely patronising to women performers and can actually work to obscure production abuses as, following the logic of this argument, if the woman smiles on screen—as in Deep Throat—can we believe there was "really" a rape? (2004: 33)

I have quoted Boyle at such length because her critique is representative of the hesitations a number of feminists feel concerning MacKinnon's broad brush. In particular, as it stands MacKinnon's analysis denies the women in pornography any agency. She fails to recognize that for these women, performing in pornography can be an attractive alternative to prostituting themselves on the street. While not denying that as attested to by Linda Marchiano, many women are violently coerced into performing in pornography, I think MacKinnon has divorced her analysis from the lived experience of the women she describes. If that is the case, then MacKinnon has strayed from the very grounding of feminist politics that she promotes.

BUTLER ON MACKINNON

MacKinnon's analysis has been challenged from a number of positions. Perhaps her most sustained and far-reaching critic is Judith Butler. Here I will attempt to present the kernel of Butler's thought, particularly as it relates to MacKinnon's writings on pornography and hate speech.

Whereas MacKinnon sees gender as a social construct, for Butler gender is performative, that is, Butler's analysis sees gender as changeable and as something one does oneself, rather than as entirely socially determined. Chris Atmore suggests that this difference means that while the postmodernist (Butler) and radical feminist (MacKinnon) understandings share much, the former position indicates that the "gender dichotomy as we tend to know it can be, and indeed already is being, disrupted, to a greater extent than radical feminism would allow" (1999: 202–203). In other words, Butler views gender as less determinist than does MacKinnon. Atmore ponders whether this postmodernist stance could "open up at least some space to address the limitations of radical feminist analysis, while building on its strengths" (1999: 203). By this formulation, radical and postmodernist feminism, as personified by MacKinnon and Butler, are not diametrical opposites. Rather, the latter is a development of the former.

In *Only Words* MacKinnon examines the Hill/Thomas affair. During Senate hearings to confirm Clarence Thomas's elevation to the U.S. Supreme Court, law professor Anita Hill testified that Thomas had sexually harassed her ten years previously when she served as his clerk. Hill's testimony was discounted and Thomas was confirmed. By MacKinnon's reading, in speaking the sexual words by which Thomas abused her, Hill became a sexual object and hence a person without credibility. MacKinnon writes: "When speech is sex, it determines what is taken as real" (1993b: 64). In MacKinnon's view, so thoroughly was Hill's testimony discounted that, in the words of Patricia Williams, Hill was said to be "consciously lying but fantasizing truth" (quoted at 1993b: 65).

MacKinnon mentions, but does not fully explore, the intersection of racism and sexism in the Senate's treatment of Anita Hill. Here we have a black woman describing a black man's sexual practices before an audience largely made of white men. Is it any wonder her speech was pornographized? Butler, on the other hand, emphasizes race. She writes:

> Yet MacKinnon uses Hill as the "example" of such sexualization without considering the relation between racialization and exemplification. In other words, it is not only that Hill is doubly oppressed, as African-American and as a woman, but that race becomes a way to represent sexuality pornographically. Just as the racialized scene of Thomas and Hill allows for the externalization of sexual degradation, so it permits for a purification in prurience for the white imaginary. African-American status permits for a spectacularization of sexuality and a recasting of whites as outside the fray, witnesses and watchers who have circuited their own sexual anxieties through the publicized bodies of blacks. (1997: 83)

Thus for Butler the *context* of Hill's speech is central whereas MacKinnon restricts her focus to the *content* of Hill's speech.

Though neither of them use the term, both MacKinnon and Butler point to the rape myth in pornography and in everyday speech. That myth holds that when a woman says "no," she really means "yes." Butler calls this the "performative contradiction," which she defines as "an act of speech that in its very acting produces a meaning that undercuts the one it purports to make" (1997: 84). While MacKinnon describes how Professor Hill's "no" was converted to the pornographic "yes," Butler again criticizes her for not recognizing the racialized context of Hill's speech:

> This account of the "structure" of pornography, however, cannot account for the context of Hill's speech act; it is not regarded as communicative, but a racialized sexual spectacle. She is the "example" of pornography because, as black, she becomes the spectacle for the projection and living out of white sexual anxiety. (1997: 84)

Moving now from the specifics of the Hill/Thomas case to MacKinnon's more general theory of pornography as hate speech, Butler questions whether pornography both represents and enacts an injury. She juxtaposes a pornographic text to a burning cross in front of a black family's house and suggests that the theory of representation and the theory of performativity differ in each case. She doubts that visual pornography can "threaten," "demean" or "debase" women in the way a burning cross does blacks. Equating these is not only erroneous but "the exploitation of the sign of racial violence for the purposes of enhancing the putatively injurious power of pornography" (1997: 21). Here I must disagree with Butler and side with MacKinnon. Like MacKinnon, I would argue that all women are affected by what is done to some women in visual pornography. Pornography is educative; it teaches men about male and female sexuality, about what men do and what women are for. In many cases to this sexual script is added a racial one: black women in chains, Japanese women in poses of deathlike passivity. Just as pornography makes misogyny sexy, it also makes racism sexy. The central message of pornography is that all women are at all times sexually available to men. Pornography renders women as sexual objects, things to be used, kept or discarded. It teaches men that a woman's "no" really means "yes." And men, particularly young men, who are the primary consumers of pornography, learn these lessons not just with their minds but with their bodies. A political text—the inferiority of women to men—is conditioned to a physical experience of arousal. As Cole comments,

> what is sexual about the way sexual ideology works is that it does not operate on the "idea" level. It works in our bodies. That is why pornography is more than just speech. It says something but it is designed specifically to elicit a physical response. (1995: 40–41)

Or, as MacKinnon summarizes, "an erection is neither a thought nor a feeling, but a behaviour" (1993b : 16).

As a final note, Butler accuses MacKinnon of seeking to increase state power at the expense particularly of gays and lesbians. She writes:

> Similarly, MacKinnon's appeal to the state to construe pornography as performative speech and, hence, as injurious conduct of

representation, does not settle the theoretical question of the relation between representation and conduct, but collapses the distinction in order to enhance the power of state intervention over graphic sexual representation. (1997: 22)

I am not convinced that MacKinnon's proposals enhance the power of the state. Indeed, as shall be demonstrated in a subsequent chapter on interventions, MacKinnon, with Dworkin, advocates empowering women to occupy the vacuum of state power. Their definition of pornography moves away from traditional notions of obscenity—a moral field adjudicated by the state—toward an encapsulation of harm experienced by women in pornography and upon whom pornography is used. And, crucially, their proposal for a model ordinance (a civic remedy to address the harm done by pornography) leaves the triggering mechanism not to state agents such as customs officers, but to women in the community.

To say that pornography encourages men's sex/sexual violence does not negate the agency of the individual perpetrator. In the first instance, men choose to consume pornography. Sometimes that choice is predicated on a wish to harm women. What I have in mind is rapists who report using pornography as a stimulus to rape. Men choose to use pornography in part because it reinforces a gender hierarchy wherein men are dominant regardless of their socioeconomic or racial position in society. By degrading women men obtain a degree of empowerment as men. This nexus of degradation and empowerment can result in a unity of men versus women. Second, as I shall argue in the chapter on choice, many men choose to believe the message of pornography over alternative formulations of what women are. And some men choose to act out what pornography broadcasts.

CONCLUSION

The strength of MacKinnon's analysis is her resolute insistence that both gender and sexuality be understood as social, not biological, constructs. Discussing gender inequality, MacKinnon writes, "The good news is, it isn't biological" (1989: 142). Similarly, MacKinnon states that to be rapable is a social, not a biological position (1989: 178). That insistence, though, has left MacKinnon open to charges of essentialism, or at least of totalizing all human experience and existence in a single model. MacKinnon's critique of sexuality presents an enormous challenge to feminist thinkers. Though the rhetoric is sometimes overblown, and it sometimes appears she is theorizing beyond the known facts, MacKinnon nonetheless offers a way of thinking about the relationships of sexuality, gender and violence that goes beyond orthodox modes of understanding. The very radicalness of her proposals encourages—perhaps provokes—a reassessment of assumptions and understandings too often taken for granted among feminist theorists. That challenge, if nothing else, makes MacKinnon's critique an invaluable contribution to the ongoing project of understanding men's sex/sexual violence.

The above discussion of the racialized sexual speech of Anita Hill leads now to a direct discussion of the relationship of sexism to other forms of hierarchy and the eroticization of hierarchy. The conceptualization I have found to be most useful in this area is intersectionality, the topic of the next chapter.

Notes

1. As shall be discussed, MacKinnon treats sexuality as synonymous with heterosexuality. While her intent in part seems to be to subsume gay and lesbian sexualities into a larger critique, I will here present that critique as applying to heterosexuality only.

2. MacKinnon's critique of sexuality is presented in different forms in a number of venues. Two of the most widely known are articles which appear in *Signs: Journal of Women in Culture and Society*, vol. 7 (1982) and vol. 8 (1983). This quotation first appeared in the first *Signs* article. I have drawn on essays contained in *Feminism Unmodified: Discourses on Life and Law* (1987) and *Toward a Feminist Theory of the State* (1989) as providing the fullest rendering of MacKinnon's thought.

4. ON INTERSECTIONALITY AND VIOLENCE AGAINST WOMEN

I have defined gender as a constructed social relation. Its content is changeable in response to historic, cultural and material conditions and in response to other social relations such as race and class. Here I wish to explore in more depth the meaning of this definition; in particular, to trace the meanings and consequences of interacting social hierarchies for women's experience of men's sex/sexual violence. The exploration will focus on race and racism as a paradigmatic case of intersectionality.

As stated earlier, all hierarchies rest on a principle of difference and the social meanings attached thereto. Collins, it will be recalled, discusses this process in terms of biological determinism. Kum-Kum Bhavnani furthers this discussion, bringing into question the very concept of race as a biological given in the following quotation:

> Racism is a system of domination and subordination based on spurious biological notions that human beings can be fixed into racially discrete groups. It is identified as a "natural" process, and is seen to be a logical consequence of the differentiation of human beings into "races." Given that there is no sound evidence from the natural and biological sciences to justify the assumption that the human species can be divided up into separate "races," both "race" and racism come to be economic, political, ideological, and social expressions. In other words, "race" is not a social category which is empirically defined, rather it is created, reproduced, and challenged through economic, political, and ideological institutions. (1993: 27)

Sherene Razack encapsulates the created and imposed characteristic of race definitions in the term "racialized women." She explains:

> I have used the term *racialized* women to refer to women whose ethnicity, as indicated by skin colour, accent, religion, and other visible markers, denotes that they are of non-Anglo-Saxon, non-French origin. In the eyes of the dominant groups such women are raced. (1994: 896)

Writing as a woman of colour in the Canadian context, Razack identifies two socially dominant groups: people of Anglo-Saxon origin and people of French origin. Note that she distinguishes these groups. She does not, for example, refer to a single dominant group of Caucasians or people of

54

European origin. In short, Razack differentiates between Anglo-Saxon and French while maintaining that both groups occupy positions of dominance. From the perspective of people of colour and Aboriginals, this is true. From the perspective of many Quebecois, on the other hand, there is only one dominant group in Canada: Anglos. These Quebecois conceivably could point to the visible markers Razack identifies—especially accent and religion—to claim that the Quebecois too are raced in the eyes of the English-speaking Protestant majority. Yet for all the talk of a distinct society, of the Quebecois—especially the "pur laine," who trace their ancestry to original French colonialists—as a separate nation, there is to my knowledge no suggestion that the Quebecois are people of colour, a "race" in the common sense.[1] The point is this: from their position of relative dominance, the Quebecois are exempt from being or seeing themselves as raced, a privilege not enjoyed by Aboriginal peoples and people of colour in Canada.

Finally, bell hooks argues that the term "white supremacy" is to be preferred to "racism," as a more accurate reflection of the operation of race in contemporary American culture. With the end of slavery and the more recent legal dismantling of the "apartheid structure of Jim Crow" (1995: 187), racist domination by overt coercive control has given way to a subtler, pervasive ideology and value system summed up in the strategy of assimilation. In the feminist movement, in academia, in the corporate world, blacks are now welcomed but only on the condition that they think, speak, act, believe and perceive reality as the dominant whites do. As hooks puts it:

> Clearly, assimilation as a social policy upholding white supremacy was strategically an important counterdefence, one that would serve to deflect the call for radical transformation of black consciousness. Suddenly the terms for success (that is, getting a job, acquiring the means to provide materially for oneself and one's family) were redefined. It was not enough for black people to enter institutions of higher education and acquire the necessary skills to effectively compete for jobs previously occupied solely by whites; the demand was that blacks become "honorary whites," that black people assimilate to succeed. (1995: 189)

Like most commentators, Bhavnani, Razack and hooks all focus on colour racism in western cultural contexts. Yet the process of racializing or "othering" does not depend exclusively on skin colour, nor is it restricted to countries historically implicated in the slave trade. An obvious example is the former Yugoslavia. There the three largest opposing groups are all racially white. Ethnically they are Slavs. In terms of religious affiliation, where it is a factor most Croats identify as Catholic while Serbs are

Orthodox Christians and Bosniacs are Muslims. Furthermore, intermarriage has been common over several generations. A process Sheila Allen describes as "selective remembering" (1994: 89) on the part of political leaders (and echoed by most journalists) has imposed exclusive categorization that previously was not the lived experience of most Yugoslavs.[2] As Allen comments:

> Ethnicity linked to nationalism and religion is claimed to have overridden all other identities in the conflict. Other descriptions, explanations, and interpretations, in which these are used as symbols to mobilize support in struggles for political and economic dominance, are by and large ignored. (1994: 89–90)

So too in Sudan, Ireland and the Indian subcontinent the process of "othering" relies on identifiers other than skin colour. In each case, and many others worldwide, elements of history, culture and/or religion are selectively invoked as social markers defining exclusive categories in the competition for political, economic or social power.

These examples point to the difficulty of defining race and racism. More complicated still is the relationship of race (and class) to gender in feminist theory. If we begin with a basic understanding that both gender and race are socially constructed so as to accord with systems of hierarchy, how is the interaction of those constructions and systems best modelled? In an article entitled "Doing Difference," Candace West and Sarah Fenstermaker critique models that they see as based in mathematics:

> The problem is that these alternative formulations have very distinctive, yet unarticulated, theoretical implications. For instance, if we think about gender, race, and class as additive categories, the whole will never be greater (or lesser) than the sum of its parts. By contrast, if we conceive of these as multiples, the result could be larger or smaller than the added sum, depending upon where we place the signs. Geometric metaphors further complicate things, since we still need to know where those planes and axes go after they cross the point of intersection (if they are parallel planes or axes, they will never intersect at all). (1995: 9)

The common failing of these mathematical models, in the view of West and Fenstermaker, is an assumption that gender, race and class can be isolated from each other. The desire to isolate gender from race and class is understandable, inasmuch as doing so allows for tidier, more manageable theory. It is also understandable when viewed in the context of the history of feminist organizing, especially internationally. For some years the admirable aim of creating global solidarity led to a refusal to acknowledge differences among the world's women. But, though understandable, this theoretical isolation does not accord with lived experience. At the level of experience we are all always simultaneously gendered, raced[3] and classed. Furthermore, the content of each category is inscribed and proscribed by the other two. This can be readily demonstrated by reference to Sojourner Truth's famous question, "Ain't I a woman?" Being gender female carries different normative expectations, meanings and outcomes for white women and women of colour in a racist society. Equally, being race black has different normative expectations, meanings and outcomes for black women and black men in a sexist society.

In an international context, Bunie Matlanyane Sexwale points out that inasmuch as violence against women is an expression of gender relations, and inasmuch as gender is socially constructed, we can expect that forms of sex/sexual violence and their incidence will vary cross-culturally. While recognizing that violence against women is global, touching all races, cultures, state forms, classes, ages and sexual orientations, she cautions:

> That said, however, we ought to acknowledge that although many forms of violence against women are common across the board, some forms and/or their incidence are strictly related to one's positioning in terms of the diversity of our realities, in time and space. Since gender is socially and historically constructed, violence against women, a manifestation of gender relations, of power relations, is therefore necessarily responsive to these diverse realities. For instance, while female genital mutilation was practiced in Europe until about the 1930s, today it occurs in isolated cases, yet it is currently widespread in parts of Africa, among certain groups. Similarly, dowry deaths and bride burning are currently specific to India, and the escalating reported cases of sexual abuse of the mentally disabled and the aged in care are currently a phenomenon of the Western world. Also, during periods of economic, political, and social upheaval and uncertainties, violence against subordinated groups, against women, often escalates. (1994: 200–201)

Razack proposes that what is needed is "an interrogation into how culture is gendered and gender is culturalized" (1994: 913). She supports this proposal in part by examining recent Canadian judicial trends in sexual assault cases where both the victim and the assailant are Aboriginal. Judges and lawyers, most of whom are white, "sometimes display a willingness to consider the history of colonization and its present-day effects as mitigating factors in the sentencing of Aboriginal males" (1994: 901). Such consciousness does not, however, extend to victims. As Razack puts it,

> What is absent here is any acknowledgment of the impact of this history of colonization and its present-day legacy on Aboriginal women as victims of sexual assault. This is how gender and race conflate to produce an absence of the realities of Aboriginal women. (1994: 901)

In this example, culture is gendered such that the history of colonization, cultural genocide, ongoing social and economic degradation on reservations, and the cycle of physical and sexual abuse begun in residential schools have differential meanings and consequences for Aboriginal men and Aboriginal women. The opposite process—by which gender is culturalized—is seen in a notorious case Razack cites: *R. v. Curley, Nagmalik, and Issigaitok*. These three Inuit men were convicted of having intercourse with a female under the age of fourteen.[4] The white judge in the case sentenced the men to only seven days, basing his leniency on information that in Inuit culture, "a young woman is deemed ready for intercourse upon menstruation" (1994: 900). In other words, the victim, an Inuk, was considered not to have suffered harm, as a white child would have. In the judge's view, the content and meaning of the category "female under the age of fourteen" is culturally specific.

In examining how culture is gendered and gender culturalized, a number of feminist writers look at the content of pornography, seeing in it motifs of the sexualization of race. Dworkin and MacKinnon, for example, discuss pornography's role in the perpetuation of racism. According to them:

> Pornography sexualizes racist hatred. It uses racially motivated violation, torture, and murder as sex acts that lead to orgasm. We believe that racist pornography is one source of the violence against black and other minorities that is ongoing in this society. We believe that it is a *dynamic* source of racist violence. (1993: 92)

This view, that sexist violence in pornography reinforces racist violence, is also put forward by Cole:

> In the pornographic universe, racism is very sexually appealing. When pornographers use black women, they place them in scenarios of slavery that fuse male dominance with racial superiority. In her chains the black pornographic female looks as if she enjoys being enslaved in both the racial and sexual senses. The pornography of Asian women is often a pornography of torture and ultra-passivity, perpetuating white western stereotypes of Asian women as passive and subservient.... Racism per se is not pornographic. Rather, pornography eroticizes racism. And one of this society's most

successful strategies for instituting values is to eroticize them. (1989: 35–36)

The racist stereotypes Cole identifies—the black woman in chains, the Asian woman so passive as to appear dead, the Jewish woman in a concentration camp—have been extensively analysed by various writers, particularly Dworkin (1981). As Collins notes, these stereotypes are not merely mental constructs; they reflect past and present practice. As she argues:

> Contemporary portrayals of black women in pornography represent the continuation of the historical treatment of their actual bodies. African-American women are usually depicted in a situation of bondage and slavery in a submissive posture, and often with two white men. (1993: 91).

In all these examples, what is described as the sexualization of race, and racism conforms to the now familiar pattern of the eroticization of inequality. It seems that domination, whether of gender or of race, is learned and experienced as sexually arousing. And, while pornography may provide the most blatant evidence, it is not the only arena in which inequality is sexualized. As Collins, drawing on political philosopher Michel Foucault, points out, sexuality is constructed at the personal level of individual consciousness and interpersonal relationships and at the structural level of social institutions. At each level, she says, "African-American women inhabit a sex/gender hierarchy in which inequalities of race and social class have been sexualized" (1993: 87).

Kimberlé Crenshaw's approach to the relationship of race and gender is to speak of "intersectionality." Interestingly, at different points she employs each of the additive, multiplicative and geometric models West and Fenstermaker find problematic. The strength of Crenshaw's reasoning, though, rests in her emphasis on the multiple dimensions of individual identity, simultaneity as lived experience, and what I will term synergistic effects of the confluence of racism and sexism. Crenshaw is critical of the tendency toward identity politics in both feminist and antiracist discourse. Identity politics frequently ignore intragroup differences. In practice this has meant that the only experiences and concerns enunciated are those of the dominant members of the group—white women in feminist politics and black men in antiracist politics. Additionally, feminist politics and antiracist politics often proceed as if on mutually exclusive terrains. In consequence, "when the practices expound identity as woman or person of colour as an either/or proposition, they relegate the identity of women of colour to a location that resists telling" (1995: 333).

The problem goes beyond the marginalization of women of colour in feminist and antiracist discourse, serious though that is. By failing to take account of the experiences of women of colour, feminist theory and antiracist theory fail in their primary tasks of analysing the operations of sexism and racism respectively. As Crenshaw summarizes:

> The problem is not simply that both discourses fail women of colour by not acknowledging the "additional" issue of race or of patriarchy but that the discourses are often inadequate even to the discrete tasks of articulating the full dimensions of racism and sexism. Because women of colour experience racism in ways not always the same as those experienced by men of colour and sexism in ways not always parallel to experiences of white women, antiracism and feminism are limited, even on their own terms. (1995: 337)

In describing the relationship of gender and race as intersectional and, more particularly, in reminding us that intersectionality is not simply a theoretical construct but lived experience, Crenshaw emphasizes that intersectional experience "is greater than the sum of racism and sexism" (1989: 140). She acknowledges that black women share experiences of discrimination with white women; they also share experiences with black men. Additionally, though, black women experience "double-discrimination—the combined effects of practices that discriminate on the basis of race and on the basis of sex. And sometimes, they experienced discrimination as black women—not the sum of race and sex discrimination, but as black women" (1989: 149).

It is this last category which leads me to think of synergism. In the realm of pharmaceuticals, many drugs are known to interact synergistically, multiplying effects exponentially. For example, most sedatives, if taken with alcohol, produce a depressive effect far in excess of their combined action. Furthermore, taken together some drugs will produce effects not present at all when taken alone. Thus, one of the theories put forward to explain the so-called Gulf War Syndrome is that it resulted from the cocktail of drugs military personnel were given to protect them from exposure to both chemical and biological weapons. In discussing experiences of double discrimination and, more especially, experiences of specific discrimination as black women, I think Crenshaw is describing the synergistic effect of the interaction of sexism and racism.

Support for this interpretation can be found in Crenshaw's explication of the meaning of white on black rape. She writes: "When Black women were raped by white males, they were being raped not as women generally, but as Black women specifically. Their femaleness made them sexually vulnerable to racist domination, while their Blackness effectively denied them any protection" (1989: 158-9). Thus for black women, it is sometimes the case that racism exacerbates sexism and sexism exacerbates racism. This dynamic interaction generates violence as a complex fusion in which the two elements cannot be separated. Such violence may be of an intensity far in excess of the additive value of the two elements and, just as importantly, it may be qualitatively different from single-axis oppression or violence. Again, pornography provides examples of the qualitative difference. MacKinnon comments that "each woman is in pornography as the embodiment of her particularities" (1996: 53). What is done to black women, to Asian women, to Latinas, to Jewish women is specific, the abuses qualitatively distinguishable from each other.

Crenshaw's description of black women's experience of violence by white men is echoed by both Radford and Kelly. Radford writes that for black women, "racism and misogyny are often inseparable dimensions of the violence" (1992: 8). And Kelly states:

> In fact, multiple levels of oppression may fuse into a complex totality which makes their separation problematic in both theory and individual experience. This is reflected in Ruth Hall's discussion of "racist sexual violence" where she argues that, for black women, assaults by white men often involve the fusion of racial and sexual violence. (1988: 29)

Finally, Sexwale, writing of black female domestic workers in South Africa, suggests that race, gender and class interact dynamically as a series of oppositions so as to increase the woman's vulnerability to violence. As Sexwale phrases it, "The dialectical combination of the varying aspects of their oppression renders domestic workers extremely vulnerable to forms of violence which permeate life and labour relations" (1994: 201).

The above quotations all refer to the case of black women assaulted by white men. There, the simultaneity and synergistic action of gender and race seem plain. But what of situations in which both the victim and the assailant are of a subordinated race? West and Fenstermaker argue that *all* social interactions, regardless of the participants or the outcome, are simultaneously gendered, raced and classed (1995: 13). We should expect, therefore, that race is always relevant to experiences of sex/sexual violence and may at times interact synergistically with gender even when the victim and the assailant share a race category. In *R. v. Curley, Nagmalik, and Issigaitok*, described above, the victim's race interacted with her gender both in the treatment accorded her by the court and in the assault itself. Customary belief that her first menstrual cycle signals an Inuk girl's sexual availability suggests that it was the combination of gender and race which resulted in the child being targeted. Presumably, these men would not have assaulted either a white girl or an Inuk boy.

Crenshaw describes a more subtle interplay of gender and race in the experiences of immigrant women beaten by their husbands. In the United States, many Asian women live in extended families, leaving them no privacy to use the telephone and no opportunity to leave the house alone. Additionally, many immigrant women fear that if they leave their husbands or even report the abuse, they will lose their residency status and so be subject to deportation. The problem is all the more acute when the family does not have legal status. Threatening deportation is a common means of abusive control used by these men. Even when the threats are groundless, if the women have no independent access to legal information and advice they will be intimidated. Finally, language barriers can make both information and services such as transition houses inaccessible to non-English-speaking women. Crenshaw concludes: "Intersectional subordination need not be intentionally produced; in fact, it is frequently the consequence of the imposition of one burden that interacts with preexisting vulnerabilities to create yet another dimension of disempowerment" (1995: 336).

The intersection of racism and sexism also has a bearing on women's willingness to speak of the violence done to them and on how their speech is received. Razack, for example, suggests that "Racialized women who bring sexual violence to the attention of white society risk exacerbating the racism directed at both men and women in their communities; we risk, in other words, deracializing our gender and being viewed as traitors, women without community" (1994: 896). Crenshaw also attributes silence to a wish to protect family and community. This may take the form of avoiding issues that might "reinforce distorted public perceptions" (1995: 340) of black men as exceptionally violent, or it may be an unwillingness to "subject their private lives to the scrutiny and control of a police force that is frequently hostile" (1995: 341). And like Razack, she points to the risk of being seen as a traitor, citing attacks made on Alice Walker for depicting a black woman abused by a black man in her novel *The Color Purple* (1995: 340).

MacLeod and Saraga combine this theme of community protection with one of internalized racism. Their description of the conflict facing a black child who has been sexually abused in the family is tragic:

> In a racist society, it is extremely important to be aware of the injustice into which a Black family may be delivered in invoking criminal proceedings, in taking children into care and in separating children and families. If the family has a central place in people's identity, how much more so for Black people for whom it may be one of the few places of retreat from racism. It is also necessary to recognize the impact that racism can have on the meaning of the event. A Black child who has internalized racism may equate being black with being bad, and the guilt that all abused children experience may confirm those feelings. She may also find it harder to "tell," since it may feel like an even greater betrayal of her family than it is to a white child. (1988: 44–45)

Finally, intersectionality plays out in situations in which the victim and the assailant are each subordinate on different axes, as for example, a black man assaulting a white woman. Klein argues that "sexual warfare often becomes a stand-in for class and racial conflict by transforming these resentments into misogyny" (1981: 72). She supports this contention by quoting a man included in Russell's *The Politics of Rape*. The man describes feeling irritated by a woman acting out her class privilege. He then describes what amounts to revenge-rape:

> I didn't really feel the urge. As a matter of fact, I had a hell of a time getting an erection.... But I forced myself to do it to prove a point to her, to prove that she wasn't as big as she thought she was. (Russell 1975: 253 quoted in Klein 1981: 72).

In the 1960s American black liberationists Eldridge Cleaver and Imama Amiri Baraka (LeRoi Jones) advocated that black men rape white women as a revolutionary act of revenge. No doubt they were responding in part to the American history of lynching—in which black men accused of making sexual advances toward white women were tortured, mutilated and killed. Note, though, that Cleaver and Baraka did not advocate exacting revenge directly against those responsible for lynching—white men. This may be interpreted as conforming to a pattern (also seen in war rape) of women's bodies being used as a means through which one group of men gets at another group of men. It may also be the case that contemporary black American men particularly resent white women as instigators of false accusations (an historically questionable claim). There is, though, a third interpretation put forward by MacKinnon: that the history of lynching itself acted to sexualize the intersection of gender female and race white in the eyes of black men, making "white girlishness ... a site of lust, hatred, and hostility" (1996: 51 n. 15). Cleaver's autobiographical writings strongly lend themselves to this interpretation. He speaks of the white woman as "The Ogre" whose psychic power over him is his "unfreedom" (1969: 6). More particularly, he describes looking at a photograph of the young white woman with whom Emmett Till was said to have flirted, an action which led to Till's murder by white men:

> While looking at the picture, I felt that little tension in the center of my chest I experience when a woman appeals to me. I was disgusted and angry with myself. Here was a woman who had caused the death of a black, possibly because, when he looked at her, he also felt the same tensions of lust and desire in his chest—and probably for the same general reasons that I felt them. It was all unacceptable to me. I looked at the picture again and again, and in spite of everything and against my will and the hate I felt for the

woman and all that she represented, she appealed to me. I flew into a rage at myself, at America, at white women, at the history that had placed those tensions of lust and desire in my chest. (1969: 11)

Cleaver's hatred and desire, projected outward and symbolized by The Ogre, leads him "as a matter of principle" to adopt "an antagonistic, ruthless attitude toward white women" (1969: 13). This in turn brings Cleaver to rape as an "insurrectionary act" (1969: 14). In his words:

I became a rapist. To refine my technique and *modus operandi*, I started out by practicing on black girls in the ghetto ... and when I considered myself smooth enough, I crossed the tracks and sought out white prey. I did this consciously, deliberately, willfully, methodically—though looking back I see that I was in a frantic, wild, and completely abandoned frame of mind. (1969: 14)

As a final comment, many black male writers describe the experience of racial oppression as emasculating and view violence as a means of restoring masculinity. Thus Cleaver writes: "We shall have our manhood. We shall have it or the earth will be leveled by our attempts to gain it" (1969: 61). Frantz Fanon states: "At the level of individuals, violence is a cleansing force. It frees the native from his inferiority complex and from his despair and inaction; it makes him fearless and restores his self-respect" (1967: 74). And if violence restores masculinity, how much more so will sexual violence directed at racially dominant women? According to Fanon:

The look that the native turns on the settler's town is a look of lust, a look of envy; it expresses his dreams of possession—all manner of possession: to sit at the settler's table, to sleep in the settler's bed, *with his wife if possible*. (1967: 30, emphasis added)

CONCLUSION

To review, race and gender intersect in experiences of violence in situations of white on black assault, situations where both the victim and the assailant are of a subordinated race, and situations of black on white assault. We have seen that race and gender sometimes interact synergistically to produce violence which may be greatly intensified, qualitatively different, or both. Can intersectionality generally, and synergism specifically, be operationalized? In other words, is it possible to develop a formula by which the effects of racism and sexism in women's experience of violence can be measured?

One of the problems with arithmetic models of the relationship of gender and race is that they assume oppression can be quantified in an absolute sense. These models also assume that a standard unit of measurement, can be arrived at so as to compare oppressions. In the case of intersectionality, we face a further problem of the fused nature of such violence. In any particular instance of violence, how are we to assign value: two parts racism, one part sexism or whatever? Precisely because racism and sexism interact dynamically to create a complex totality, the effect of each cannot be separated out either in theory or in the lived experience of individuals. From situation to situation the participants' respective race categories, gender categories and class categories may be stressed or muted but they are all always present. As West and Fenstermaker put it, "The point is that how we label such dynamics does not necessarily capture their complex quality. Foreground and background, context, salience, and centre shift from interaction to interaction, but all operate interdependently" (1995: 33). In sum, intersectionality and synergism are useful theoretical constructs for understanding the dynamic relationship of forms of oppression, but they cannot be applied formulaically.

Let us consider a final point. Crenshaw maintains that white feminists often "ignore how their own race functions to mitigate some aspects of sexism and, moreover, how it often privileges them over and contributes to the domination of other women" (1989: 154). Are white women less vulnerable to men's sex/sexual violence than women of colour? Sometimes racism interacts synergistically with sexism. In many cases a woman is targeted for abuse both for her gender and for her race. Sometimes the intensity of racist sexual violence is greater than single-axis violence. However, social statuses other than gender and race also sometimes increase an individual's exposure to risk. Poverty, for example, may leave one more vulnerable to certain forms of street violence. It is also a factor in trapping some women in systems of prostitution and pornography. Mental or physical disability may increase the chance of victimization, as may incarceration in hospitals, prisons, residential or reform schools and foster care facilities. Perhaps most importantly, prior victimization, especially in childhood, seems to escalate the likelihood of further abuse. As MacKinnon puts it, "skin privilege ... has never insulated white women from the brutality and misogyny of men, mostly but not exclusively white men, or from its effective legalization" (1996: 52). In the international context, Barry points out that "it is useless and destructive for women to compare the relative advantages of one form of sexual slavery over another, in an allegiance to a particular culture" (1979: 195). The same is true, it seems to me, within a given culture or state.

Feminists have learned the importance of acknowledging differences in women's experiences, of theorizing ways gender interacts with other social statuses to create a totality of experience. In accounting for difference, though, it is important neither to represent a hierarchy of oppression among women nor to lose sight of the main issue. As Hanmer, Radford and Stanko put it, "Other power structures mean women can be simultaneously privileged and oppressed ... *but all men by virtue of their gender have power as men in relation to all women*" (1989a: 6–7, emphasis added).

Notes

1. I am drawn to speculate on the significance of the title of a text which powerfully influenced the early Quebec separatist movement: *White Niggers of America*, by Pierre Vallieres. The confluence of racism and anti-francphonie is also evidenced in the expression "speak white," meaning speak English.
2. Cynthia Enloe points out that this remembering is masculine: "Nationalism typically has sprung from masculinized memory, masculinized humiliation, and masculinized hope" (1989: 44).
3. This usage is distinct from Razack's, for whom being raced or racialized is something that is imposed on subordinate groups by the socially dominant. Here "raced" refers to assignment to and occupation of a race category, an ascriptive process undergone by all members of a society
4. Note that the statute under which these men were tried, and related articles of the Criminal Code, specify that consent is not an issue. Any sexual involvement with an underage person is *ipso facto* sexual assault.

5. VIOLENCE AS PROCESS

There is a tendency among many of us to look at violence as an event, either singular, as in a stranger rape attack, or multiple, a series of linked events as in wife battering. I am coming to think, though, that men's violence against women is better represented as a process. This process begins with the individual man's motivation and moves to action, followed by effects for the victim, for the perpetrator and for the witnesses—those who come to know of this particular set and more generally society at large. This process, of course, must be seen in the context of the hegemony of male supremacy, which condones and at times requires men to be violent toward women. It must also be seen in the context of gendered relations constituted by male supremacy. I picture this process and its embeddedness as in Figure 3.

The advantages of viewing violence as a process are first that it links social conditions and individual behaviour. In other words, violence comes to be seen not as aberrant but as typical, predictable behaviour in hegemonic masculinity and gendered relations of male dominance and female submission. Second, it then highlights the agency of perpetrators, making it plain that their violent acts are not impulsive or biologically driven but rather are subject to thinking and planning. Third, it connects violence with its consequences for victims, perpetrators and society in general.

Investigation into the motivations of violent men is an area which has not been given thorough attention in feminist research. Quite rightly, feminists have focused on the experiences of women. As we have listened to women, so it is time to listen to violent men and what they say about their attitudes and desires. Sometimes it is necessary to read backwards, at other times the men themselves give insight into what drives them by what they say and do to their victims. Here is an example taken from an early

Figure 3: Violence as Process

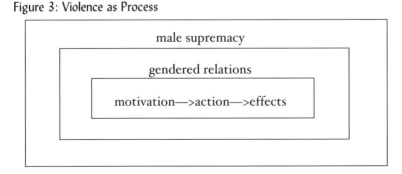

study of mine. The subject in this case is child sexual abuse:

> And what of the men? What do they say about their sexual abuse of children? Some women report that after assaulting them the abusers apologized and promised it wouldn't happen again, though of course it did. Some women say the abusers blamed them for the assaults, claiming the victim was in control or that she was a whore and wanted to be raped. For other women the abuse was passed off as sex education. Still others say their abuser claimed the victim was "special": that she was the only one who could do what he needed, that what he did to her was their shared secret, or that it was a "relationship." Some abusers characterized it as just a fun little game between them. Some women say the abuser claimed not to be responsible for their actions, that they could only respond to the imperatives of their erect penises.
>
> Finally, many women say the abusers gave no explanation. This suggests the most common reason a man sexually abuses a female child: his assumption that it is natural for him to get what he wants. As one woman put it, "because my father wanted to abuse me. That's why it happened." (Price 1989: 26–7)

Of course the analysis of men's motivations does not end with their words. Rather, those words must be illuminated by a feminist gaze that encompasses the stratified social relations noted above. Sometimes this involves taking a more distanced view than that of individual victims, as Hilary Eldridge does in listing some of what motivates men to sexually abuse children. According to Eldridge:

> Most sex offenders do sexual things to children because they want to. For some, motivation is linked more strongly to the desire to control and overpower, whereas others have a more strongly sexual motivation. Some have an emotional congruence with children linked to a sense of inadequacy with adults and seek to meet their needs for human contact by creating abusive relationships with children. Others are anger motivated, in some cases directed at children and in others at adults. Sexual arousal to the pain and suffering of another is clearly present in sadistic offenders. In a minority of cases, offenders are initially coerced or drawn into inappropriate behaviours, for example, when they are adolescent, or in the context of a residential school or home run by abusers who corrupt them. (Eldridge 2000: 317–18)

Finally, still on the subject of child sexual abuse, Ray Wyre distinguishes predatory from non-predatory paedophiles. The former "typically sexually abuse within the context of abduction, or may express immediate anger in a sexual way" (2000: 60). These are the stranger rapists we warn our children about, though as Wyre notes, they may be the rapist within the home. Non-predatory paedophiles have more complex motivations. According to Wyre, they believe

> a child can give consent to sexual acts. They believe that a child is sexual; that a child would enjoy sex with an adult, and that a child can give consent.... At the extreme end of this is the "paedophile" who believes that a baby can give consent. (2000: 61)

The above do not exhaust the list of men's motivations for sex/sexual violence. Some are idiosyncratic or exist only among some groups within a culture. The glaring and horrifying example of this category is a case that arose in South Africa recently of half a dozen men who serially raped an eighteen-month old baby in the belief that doing so would cure them of AIDS.

If we open our feminist lens to its widest aperture, we come to a definition of violence which is grounded in motivation. Dobash et al. suggest:

> The focal point in pro-feminist men's programmes is the violence. Reflecting feminist interpretations of male violence ... pro-feminist perspectives consider violence as intentional behaviour chosen by men as a tactic or resource associated with attempts to dominate, control and punish women. (2000: 293)

This chain is more specific than the one I presented earlier. Assuming the environments of male supremacy and gendered relations, this chain would look like this:

intention —> violent behaviour —> domination, control, punishment

A few things stand out in this definition. The first and most obvious is that the will to violence is a conscious one. The second is that violence is a behaviour, not a conditioned response to the environment. The third is that what I have called the effects of violent action are in this model directly linked to the motive force or intention.

A part of hegemonic masculinity, at least as a model for men, is that they attempt to consolidate power over others around them whenever they can. Yet Kaufman (1997) points out that despite the fact that men are dominant and privileged, many men do not feel dominant at all. In his words, "The process of stuffing oneself into the tight pants of masculinity is a difficult one for all men, even if it is not consciously experienced as such" (1997: 31). This contradiction, between ideology and lived experience, is not easy for individual men to resolve, but violence against women may provide that sense of empowerment that they may believe psychologically is rightfully theirs. Building on Dobash et al.'s work, we can see that violence is indeed a resource, a tool for bridging men's psychological and physical sense of power/powerlessness. What interests me most in both these models is the movement from the first element to the second. It is one thing to feel motivated to act in a particular way but quite another to actually do so, to carry out the act. That moment, represented in both chains by the first arrow, I identify as choice. A fuller discussion of feminist analyses of men's choice to do violence will follow this chapter. For now let us keep it in mind.

Moving now to the violent actions, these range from inappropriate sexual comments to a co-worker through to sexual mutilation and femicide. On the subject of wife battering, Jayne Mooney identifies five categories of violence. As summarized by Itzin, these are:

- mental cruelty, which included verbal abuse (e.g., the calling of names, being ridiculed in front of other people), being deprived of money, clothes, sleep, prevented from going out;
- threats of violence or force;
- actual physical violence, which included being grabbed or pushed, or shaken, being punched or slapped, kicked, head-butted, attempted strangulation, hit with a weapon/object;
- physical injury, which included bruising or black eyes, scratches, cuts, bites, broken bones, being burned with cigarettes, scalded, knocked unconscious, and experiencing miscarriages as a result of an assault; and
- rape, defined as being made to have sex without consent involving actual violence or its threat. (Itzin 2000c: 357)

By my schema (Figure 3), Mooney's physical injuries categories would belong under "effects." Aside from that caveat, the list is impressive in providing a sense of the range of violent acts men inflict on their wives/partners.

Cathy Winkler (1995) used her resources as an ethnographer, a teacher of Women's Studies and a volunteer rape crisis counsellor to survive a three and a half hour ordeal at the hands of a stranger rapist. The attack was planned, as evidenced by the rapist's boast that he had been watching her for three weeks, had loosened a basement window some time before the night of his attack and had entered her home on a previous evening but retreated on hearing Winkler on the telephone. Not only was the attack planned, it was purposeful. Winkler suggests the attacker had a cluster of motivations. At the risk of decontextualization, I will list them here:

Robbers do not wake up their victims. In the case of this rapist, it was important for me to be awake, because it was my reactions to the terror that provided his enjoyment. (1995: 161)

Rapists desire the victim's subjugation.... When I complied, I had demonstrated my subordination to his desires, and *that* was his goal. (1995: 161)

His contortions with my body were his forms of "pleasure." Paining me pleasured him. (1995: 165)

Rapists are addicts of dictatorial power. Their needles are their victims, who are seen as valued commodities. Without us, rapists cannot feel drugged or exuberant. (1995: 170)

The robbery of money had many meanings. First, this is how he makes his living. He had said, "I'm a robber." Second, my cash payment to him for the rapes was another mechanism of his power. He enjoyed my subjugation, and he enjoyed the fact that the victim had paid for her own humiliation. (1995: 171)

The rapist beat Winkler viciously, pulverizing her head and face, throwing her against a wall with such intensity that he broke her back open, and forcing her to lie with his weight on her on a bed strewn with broken glass. He raped her vaginally, orally and anally. He also forced her to lick his anus. This rather bald repetition of the "facts" cannot come close to capturing the viciousness of the rapist's attack nor the terror it/he instilled in Winkler. It also fails to convey Winkler's agency—the thinking, speaking and acting which probably saved her life. My purpose in including it is to give a picture of stranger rape as a suffusion of sex and violence in which the two components cannot be separated. I will return to this account when discussing effects.

Finally, Jan Barnsley and Pamela Sleeth argue that men's sex/sexual violence should not be separated from its effects. They are concerned that publishing first person accounts of child sexual abuse may provide abusers with material to "get off on" (1989: 76), a concern Winkler also expresses. Using the words "acts" and "consequences," they provide a sample of the experience of child sexual abuse, drawn from children's disclosure statements and their mothers' reports of physical and behavioural changes, and the recollections of adult survivors. While they do not do so, I will present some of their excerpts in two categories: immediate effects and long-term effects. All italics and ellipses are in the original.

Oral sex with ejaculation ... she said "tongue swollen up, Daddy

took his pee-pee out. I had to swallow my spit. Daddy was hurt—
he was saying oh oh."

Cut her own tongue with scissors; cut her hair and her sister's hair in big chunks. Threw dishes on the floor, wrecked furniture, ran in front of cars, walked up to strangers and hit them, played with matches... (1989: 77)

Daddy pinches me right here [vaginal area]...

Urinary tract infection, throwing up, rubbing herself violently. Very quiet. Screamed if you touched her. Wears layers of clothes on a hot summer day. Lies in bed and shakes, says she never sleeps, covers up tightly to stop shivering... (1989: 78)

When I was young, he did a lot of things in front of the family; French kissing, fondling. Later it was regular intercourse. At age ten the sex got more and more violent and that's when I started to get hurt. It got perverse. I don't know what he used—he had dental instruments—I was different from something he was wanting—he put them inside me.

Constant bleeding inside, rectally, scar tissue ... scared of the instruments ... I definitely feared him. Concerned I'd get pregnant. I have bad dreams about his office and the paraphernalia ... I was ostracized from everybody. I just didn't want to exist. I started to emotionally abuse people. I wanted people to hurt ... I did a lot of drinking, a lot of drugs ... I haven't cried since I was nine years old, my feelings were apart from me. (1989: 79)

I have memories from when I was in the crib. I think I was two or under. My main memory is ... his penis in my mouth. I remember his hands and being touched genitally—never penetrated with his penis but touched.... One time when I was twelve, thirteen, I remember him coming in my mouth after genital touching, stimulation ... me feeling choked and thinking I was going to die....

Somehow I was responsible if it was happening, my being a bad person, there being something wrong with me. I spaced right out of my body, made a split to deal with things in my head. It forced me into excelling at school. Not trusting my own feelings, not trusting of other people. Difficulties being intimate. Screaming rages. Chronic back and neck problems, voice and throat constriction. Dissociating from what I'm feeling. A residue of rage. (1989: 79)

In this barest review of wife battering, rape and child sexual abuse, what comes across most clearly is the sheer variety of men's acts of sex/sexual violence. Assuming the voice of the perpetrator, we might paraphrase Austrian philosopher Ludwig Wittgenstein to say, "The limits of my imagination are the limits of my violence." Furthermore, in many cases that imagination is informed by pornography, though I do not wish to suggest that pornography "causes" men to be violent in any lockstep kind of way. Rather, pornography can provide a mental, visual, imaginary language for the physical, bodily, actual practices of men bent on abusing women and children. By way of example, in a recent case in Toronto a man named Michael Briere pleaded guilty to abducting, sexually assaulting and murdering a ten-year-old girl. Briere testified that having sex with a prepubescent child had been a fantasy "probably forever." To feed the fantasy, Briere downloaded pornographic images of ten- to twelve-year-old girls on his home and work computers as often as twice a day. Finally, on the day in question, having spent the afternoon looking at child pornography, Briere left his apartment to find a child. In his words, "And I just got excited, and just went, I needed to go out and see if I ... I just went out. I really wanted to do it" (quoted in Christie Blatchford 2004: A1). Let me be clear in stating that Briere's motivation existed prior to his consumption of child pornography. He did not "accidentally" discover child pornography on the internet but instead went searching for it. Nor did viewing child pornography inevitably lead to the kidnap, assault and murder of Holly Jones. In short, Briere acted out of choice both in viewing and acting. And to the extent that he did, he must be held accountable for his behaviour.

As was made clear by the accounts provided by Barnsley and Sleeth, the effects for victims of men's violence can be both immediate and long term, physical, emotional, mental and psychological. Similarly, Winkler describes a range of effects. During the attack she found herself dissociating, something common to many victims of violence, especially children: "I began to step outside of myself. My self was pulling away from my body. My essence wanted to get away from the body of mine that the rapist was torturing" (1995: 174). In addition to her physical injuries, she writes that in the immediate aftermath of the attack, "I felt like I was hanging from the edge of a steep cliff that represented 'sanity,' peering down into the canyon of insanity" (1995: 155). Winkler links this feeling of insanity directly to the rapist's words and actions. According to her:

> Rapists have forced V-Ss [victim-survivors] into a state of ambiguity, a chaos of insanity. As a result, the aftermath of trauma involves unexpected jolts of volcanolike eruptions of pain that unexpectedly and unpredictably surface, resurface and keep resurfacing. Moreover, because the rapist has stabbed the identity of V-Ss multiple times, the impact leaves V-Ss, like myself, to experience lengthy periods

of intense crying in which we mourn the loss of part of ourselves. (1995: 177)

Finally, Winkler summarizes her responses as dissociation, emotional numbness and rape trauma (1995: 176).

Winkler makes clear that whether deliberately or not, the rapist's words and actions create this sense of impending insanity. For example, Winkler's attacker attempted to make her responsible for the beating he meted out: "You made me do it. It's your fault. I didn't want to hurt you" (1995: 169). This false ascription of blame is also very common among men who batter their wives/partners. To take just two examples, Dobash et al. quote a man saying, "Well, I wasn't trying to strangle her—but she was fighting back—but I had my hand round her throat and I had one hand trying to hold [daughter]" (2000: 16). Another man claims in justification: "Well, if she'd let me do it [have sex] I wouldn't have punched her" (2000: 30). Blaming the victim is also common among men who sexually abuse children as my earlier discussion makes clear.

Winkler describes the rapist's words making her feel like a prostitute, "a professional in the pleasures of male sexual performance" (1995: 169). In this Winkler echoes Inger Agger's analysis of the sexualization of the political technology of the female body, by which she means that the female body is made sexual in a political economy that demands of it both production and obedience. Agger suggests that one of the functions of torture is to "disgrace its victim by disgracing her body" (1994: 69). Drawing on the work of philosopher Agnes Heller on the power of shame, she argues that to the extent that the prostitute is viewed as a symbol of shame, the fundamental goal of torture is to "turn the woman into a whore" (1994: 72). Margaret Gordon and Stephanie Riger also speak of the shame that comes from the sexualization of violence in rape in western cultures. According to them:

> To show power and anger through rape—as opposed to mugging or assault—men are calling on lessons women learn from society, from history and religion, to defile, degrade and shame in addition to inflicting physical pain. Rapists have learned, *as have their victims,* that to rape is to do something worse than to assault. (1989: 45, quoted in Helliwell 2000: 791, emphasis in original)

Turning now to the effects of violent actions on the men who perpetrate them, what stands out most clearly is pleasure. Some of this has been previously discussed in the treatment of motivations, for example, Winkler's assertion that "paining me pleasured him" (1995: 165). Deborah Cameron also writes of the pleasure of inflicting pain, though her analysis is somewhat more nuanced. She writes:

It is this feeling of absolute power and freedom which affords pleasure, including and indeed particularly sexual pleasure. The dependence of pleasure on mastery over another is the link feminist analysts perceive between the extreme behaviour of sexual murders and "normal" masculinity. (1999: 78)

Jalna Hanmer identifies pleasure as an effect of interpersonal violence and links it to studies of pleasure in war and other extreme political circumstances. She writes:

Men express many feelings through violence and their feelings may determine their actions. *Many men enjoy inflicting violence....* Knowledge of this type of personal behaviour is well documented in the study of war and political regimes in which torture and genocide are part of the social process, but it has yet to be incorporated into family studies. (2000: 12, emphasis added)

Following Hanmer's lead, I will here present some of Johanna Bourke's work on face-to-face killing in modern warfare. Following a discussion of American soldiers in Vietnam debating the relative enjoyment of napalm versus white phosphorus, Bourke writes: "The experience seemed to resemble spiritual enlightenment or sexual eroticism: indeed, slaughter could be likened to an orgasmic, charismatic experience. However you look at it, war was a 'turn on'" (1999: 15). Bourke quotes Philip Caputo writing that killing in war is like "getting screwed for the first time" and gave men "an ache as profound as the ache of orgasm" (1999: 32). American soldiers who first raped then killed their female victims were approvingly named "double veterans" (1999: 175) and the opportunity to rape was "an inducement to encourage Marines to volunteer for Vietnam" (Chuck Onan cited at 191). Nor are such attitudes restricted to American men in Vietnam; Maja Korac quotes a Serbian paramilitary on his return from the Croatian front saying the most interesting aspects of being a soldier are "shooting and fucking" (quoted in Korac 1996: 137).

For most western men, war is exceptional, something viewed in the movie theatre and on television news broadcasts. Even at this distance, however, war can be a motive force for men's sex/sexual violence against women. Various commentators, including Korac (1996: 138) and Mrsevic and Hughes (1997: 120) have identified what has been dubbed the "post-TV News syndrome" in Serbia during the Yugoslav wars. This describes a pattern of men beating their wives or mothers after watching violent, hate-filled propaganda on television. It must be stressed that this is not "front-line" violence and that the victims of this violence are, in the eyes of the perpetrators, "Our Women." Another example comes from Canada's Maritime region, where during the first Gulf War, shelter workers reported men dressing up in combat uniforms before battering their wives (Kelly 2000:59).

Hannah Arendt teaches that "the practice of violence, like all action, changes the world, but the most probable change is to a more violent world" (1970: 80). This is as true of men's sex/sexual violence as it is for the kind of inter- and intra-state violence Arendt had in mind. Each news report of a stranger rapist, each TV movie of the week focusing on wife-battering, each home-grown pornographic image of a child released on the internet serves to make the world a more dangerous place for women and children. This often prurient publicity has two effects: it encourages men to act on their violent desires; and it encourages women to accept men's violence, even to feel responsible for it. By way of example, when Peter Sutcliffe was terrorizing West Yorkshire, senior police figures proposed a curfew for women. Never mind that a curfew for men would have been more to the point, the barely concealed subtext was that women are responsible for men's violence, that Sutcliffe's victims "asked for it" by being out alone without the protection of a man.

The mainstreaming of violence against women into popular culture is vividly illustrated in the following vignette by Irish feminist Ailbhe Smyth:

> On 17 January last, an ordinary Tuesday, I decided to spend an ordinary evening watching TV. I like watching TV. I had a "choice" in the 9 to 10 pm slot: a "thriller" about the so-called aggravated rape and murder of a woman; a "chiller" about a nurse who fears her husband is a serial killer; a "drama" about a husband's psychological and physical abuse of his wife and children, and his subsequent murder by his wife; an episode of "Law and Order" about a young black girl's "controversial" claim to have been raped by a white policeman. I didn't want to "choose" any of these, because watching programmes like these make me more, not less, nervous. I don't want to see fictional representations of how men brutalise women, because they are for all the world (to see) indistinguishable from the "real thing" I hear about and read about every day of my life. I don't find representations of women as bad or mad, or stupid or victimised at all entertaining. However "puritanical" it makes me sound, however "unscientific" my thinking, however unsophisticated and literal my analysis, I can't seem to stop worrying about the relationship between what we see, how we see it and what we do. My alternative "choice" that evening was a documentary about the history of sport, entitled "Blood, Sweat and Glory." Don't tell me I'm paranoid. (1996: 64–65)

Pornography provides an even clearer example of the social and cultural effects of men's violence against women. Women and children are harmed in the production of pornography whether that production is commercial or home grown. In turn other women and children are harmed in being forced to consume pornography. And women and children are harmed in being forced to enact scenarios depicted in pornography. At the same time, pornography motivates and instructs men to commit violence against women and children and to justify this behaviour. It teaches men what a woman is "for" and what it means to be a man in a system of male supremacy. It conditions desire. More particularly, pornography conditions a physiological response (arousal) to scenes of violence and degradation. Men learn, not just with their minds but with their bodies, the lessons of male and female sexuality contained in pornography.

Some feminist writers view the effects of men's sex/sexual violence as a kind of deliberate conspiracy among men. An early example comes in the introduction to Brownmiller's *Against Our Will* in which she claims that rape is "nothing more or less than a conscious process by which *all* men keep *all* women in a state of fear" (1975: 15). While accepting that all men benefit from the rapist's actions, and all women suffer, I am not convinced that this process is conscious. I do not accept the notion of a grand male conspiracy. There does not need to be, for the institution and ideology of male supremacy allows men to act unreflexively in their abuse of women and children and in their support of other men who are abusive.

Finally, violence for men acts as a feedback loop such that the effects of power, dominance, control and sexual gratification reinforce the original motivations of violence. In turn the violence escalates, becoming addictive. For the individual perpetrator, what started as a push becomes a slap which becomes a punch. Similarly, a consumer of pornography may move from *Hustler* to *Snuff*. And so violence is normalized in the minds of men and the experiences of women. The process of violence becomes a closed circle. In the next chapter I will consider where that circle might be interrupted.

6. CHOICE AND ACCOUNTABILITY

INTRODUCTION

This chapter is premised on an assumption that evil is neither mysterious nor supernatural. Rather, it is a human capacity and is understandable in human terms. As much as we, the observers, may wish to close our eyes and minds to man-made horror we have the ability, and so the obligation, to struggle to understand. Proceeding from this assumption, the analysis in this chapter has been further inspired by two sources. The first is Hannah Arendt's description of the conviction that led her to write *The Origins of Totalitarianism* in the immediate aftermath of the Holocaust. Arendt wrote:

> That this [the escalation of anti-Jewish violence] called not only for lamentation and denunciation but for comprehension seemed to me obvious. This book is an attempt at understanding what at first and even second glance appeared simply outrageous.
>
> Comprehension, however, does not mean denying the outrageous, deducing the unprecedented from precedents, or explaining phenomena by such analogies and generalities that the impact of reality and the shock of experience are no longer felt. It means, rather, examining and bearing consciously the burden that events have placed upon us—neither denying their existence nor submitting meekly to their weight as though everything that in fact happened could not have happened otherwise. Comprehension, in short, means the unpremeditated, attentive facing up to, and resisting of, reality—whatever it may be or might have been. (1979: xiv)

The second inspirational source is Max Weber's construct of *Verstehen*, or interpretive understanding,[1] which he developed out of the work of Wilhelm Dilthey and Georg Simmel. Weber maintained that the aim or purpose of an action is its cause. As Fritz Ringer puts it, "agents envisage the results they hope to achieve, along with the means of attaining these results, and that is what moves them to act" (1997: 92–93). Understanding human behaviour, then, requires an investigation of motives, not in any sort of teleological sense, but in the sense of discovering "what actually moved persons to act in particular cases" (Ringer 1997: 94).

As a mode of analysis, *Verstehen* begins from the premise that any given action has a purpose envisaged by the actor. Thus, actions are "rational" from the actor's perspective. The interpreter's task is to understand the action by comprehending the actor's subjectively intended meaning even—perhaps especially—when such action appears to diverge from logical or ethical rationality. Like Arendt, then, Weber held that even the outrageous is open to comprehension. Weber recommended that the analyst attempt to understand the world (self, other, means, resources) as it is perceived by the actor *without* identifying with the actor. In other words, interpretation does not require any correspondence between the actor's subjectivity and the interpreter's. Weber repeatedly stressed that one does not have to *be* Caesar to understand Caesar (Ringer 1997: 95). Interpretation does not, however, imply empathy. Still less does understanding lead to moral relativism or subjectivism. In short, understanding an action such as genocide is one thing, tolerating or excusing it is quite another. While not denying that the process of attaining understanding can be intellectually, emotionally and spiritually taxing, it is nevertheless both possible and necessary. This chapter assumes that the perpetrators of violence against women are not madmen or devils but ordinary men acting out of comprehensible motives.

CHOICE

It will be recalled that in the discussion of the definition of violence Dobash et al. made the point that violence is intentional. Here I wish to expand on that notion. In particular, I wish to write about choice in violence. I will begin by drawing on my own previous work related to the systematic rapes in the wars in the former Yugoslavia before turning to other feminist commentators who examine violence in more domestic settings.

Choice is central to the ascription of moral responsibility. Ratiocination—the ability to reason—underlies choice. This is why those deemed insane (a legal rather than medical designation) are not held responsible for their criminal actions. Either they were unable to appreciate consequences or they were driven to act as they did and had no power to resist. While society may legitimately protect itself from the actions of these damaged souls, it does not have the right to punish them.[2] It would be untenable, however, to argue that a form of mass psychosis was visited upon the hundreds, perhaps thousands of individual perpetrators of sexual violence in the former Yugoslavia. The question, then, is to what extent they acted out of choice.

Two arguments can be put forward in favour of the proposition that individual men rightly should be held accountable. The first argument involves access to alternative conceptualizations of women, men, sexuality and sexual violence. Catharine MacKinnon describes a young Serbian soldier who was raised in a cultural environment of pervasive pornography[3] and who first experienced sex when he raped and killed in the war. MacKinnon draws a direct, causal link between these two elements. According to her, "Pornography is the perfect preparation—motivator and instruction manual in one—for the sexual atrocities ordered in this geno-cide" (1993a: 28). If all he knew of sexuality, if all he knew of women was what he had learned from pornography, did this soldier have a choice? I think he did. He could have refused the message of pornography, even a message reinforced by government policy, military ethos and the encouragement of his fellows. If he had a mother, a sister, an aunt, a girlfriend or a female teacher, he had access to a different understanding of women than that presented in pornography. If he was raised as a Christian or as a citizen, he had access to a different message about fit social relations and behaviours. To the extent that he chose to heed one message (that of pornography) and not another, he is responsible and should be held accountable.[4]

The second argument in favour of choice, hence accountability, con-siders evidence of similarly located men—that is, subject to the same ideological forces, intragroup pressures, etc., as perpetrators—who did not sexually abuse women. But first let us hear the counter-argument, provided by Euan Hague, who says that:

> The context of group rape is particularly important in a war where failure to obey orders to rape was likely to result in death for the abstainer. There was no anonymity for the soldier coerced to gang rape. *There was no choice.* (1997: 57, emphasis added)

In spite of his claim that these men had no choice, Hague goes on to argue that they are still accountable. His concern is in apportioning blame. He suggests that while coercion does not absolve these men of their crimes, they should be seen as less culpable than the officials who dictated policy.

Against this, there is evidence of soldiers who not only refused, but actually came to the aid of victims, protecting them by various means from the sexual violence of their comrades. Here are some examples taken from various sources and testimonies:

> Then [another] soldier came in. I had never seen him before but I would like to know who he is because he saved my life. He shouted at these young soldiers and he cursed them. He said, "What are you doing to this woman?" (Human Rights Watch Vol. II, 1993: 167)

> One girl told me that an older soldier saved her life. She'd been taken to a control point in the woods and was raped there by several drunken soldiers. They were supposed to kill her afterward, but this older soldier brought her back to the camp. (Stiglmayer 1994: 91)

> The companion unsuccessfully tried to stop the volunteer, who was drunk, from raping, so he protected and hid the victim's daughter.

(Commission of Experts Annex IX 1994, para. 106)

> One of the men attempted to rape the woman of the house, but his companion stopped him. (Commission of Experts Annex IX 1994, para. 271)

It is important not to dismiss the very real, immediate physical threat under which some perpetrators felt themselves to be. Surrounded by armed men drunk on alcohol, testosterone and triumphant nationalism, men who knew that their worst excesses would be ignored (if not condoned) by their political and military masters, it is perhaps understandable that some men raped out of fear for their lives. Yet, as witnessed above, others resisted.

Even more important than the actions of "resisters," though, is what underlies those actions. These men were able to recognize that however fervently they believed in their nationalist cause, some actions were not justified. Like their fellows, resisters were immersed in an atmosphere of unbridled hatred and fear of the other and pornographic imagination, yet they realized that sexual abuse, torture and enslavement were not the actions of honourable men and soldiers. To the extent that the resisters knew these things, so could their fellows have known. To the extent that the perpetrators could have known and chose not to, or knowing acted anyway, they are responsible for their actions. As Arendt, figuratively speaking to Adolf Eichmann writes: "For politics is not like the nursery; in politics obedience and support are the same" (1964: 279).

Over the years much debate has been conducted on the origins of male violence. Leaving aside biological explanations, which were once derided but are now being reasserted by some academics, attention has focused on environmental conditions. The contested area of research into the effects of pornography is one example (cf. Boyle 2000). While important, such research carries a risk, especially when it is popularized. By way of example, some years ago researchers, feminist and otherwise, uncovered a statistically significant correlation between men who batter their wives and who had fathers who beat their mothers. This correlation was translated into a causal analysis: men learn to batter their wives by watching their fathers batter their mothers. What this analysis glosses over is batterers whose fathers were not violent and, more importantly, the sons of batterers who as adults do not beat women. The existence of these two groups suggests that the nexus of environmental conditions and subsequent adult behaviour does not entirely abrogate individual agency. A similar argument can be made regarding soldier-rapists. To suggest, as I have done, that the construction of masculinity under militarized state nationalism predisposes men to be sexually violent does not negate the agency of the individual soldier-rapist. And where there is agency there must be responsibility.

Some men eschew the violence of their fathers. Some soldiers do not rape "enemy" women. Exposed to the same environmental conditions as other men, these men demonstrate that in the final analysis choice is always available.

It is not possible to "prove" in any absolute sense that the men who raped women during the war in the former Yugoslavia did so out of choice. Very few men have admitted their deeds. Of those who have, most blame others, saying, for example, that they were just "following orders." The defence of following orders has not been accepted by the International Criminal Tribunal for the Former Yugoslavia nor, I think, should it be. In any event, while we cannot know directly what prompted these men to rape, we can interpret their words and behaviours and extrapolate from the behaviour of their fellows who did not rape. More research is needed into why some men rape in wartime and especially into why others do not. Are there differences of age, rank, socialization, religious devotion? Are some men immune to ideological hegemony and if so, why? Of the men who rape in war, how do they explain their actions to themselves? On returning from "action" do they boast to their fellows or silently drink themselves into a stupor? The questions arising are multiple. For now, based on the evidence presented above, we can conclude that in most cases even in wartime rape is a discretionary power.

So much for rape in war. That situation is, at least for most western men, an exceptional one. What of the far more common setting of violence in the home and local community? Itzin is blunt and categorical when she states: "This is what men do because they want to; because they can; and because largely, they get away with it." (2000a: 5) In another piece on child sexual abuse Itzin expands on this statement, saying:

> It is necessary to recognize that there is no solution to the problem without addressing the "men thing" of it, the matter of men wanting it and doing it and largely getting away with it, and nothing effective being done to stop them. It is necessary to understand that child sexual abuse won't end until the men who want it and do it decide to stop it; and the men who don't want it or do it decide to stop the men who do. (Itzin 2000b: 448)

This quotation succinctly summarizes the state of feminist analysis specifically about child sexual abuse but also about violence against women and children generally. Itzin identifies three elements necessary for any solution to the problem of child sexual abuse. First is the "men thing" of it, which speaks to incidence. Most reliable studies suggest that in 90 percent of cases of the sexual abuse of children, the perpetrator is male. Second, Itzin includes in the "men thing" getting away with it, which is a commentary on the current state of child protection laws and agencies as well as a cultural norm of acceptance of male sexuality (at least in its heterosexual mode) regardless of how abusive its expression is. Third, accordingly, Itzin's proposed solution mirrors her analysis: abusers must stop abusing and other men must stop condoning them.

It has been increasingly popular both in academia and in the mainstream media to pathologize the behaviour of men who are sexually violent toward women and children. One effect of this trend has been to shift responsibility away from abusers. Kelly, Regan and Burton write:

> The focus on sexual arousal moves us into further difficulties since the recent emphasis on individual men choosing to act or not act and having to take responsibility for those choices is much more difficult to sustain where "arousal" is represented as the biological/ essential element within individuals. (2000: 78)

Clinical practice with offenders suggests that contrary to the picture of an instinct-driven sex beast, abusers often plan their abuse, identify their victim(s), groom them, isolate them from non-offending adults and so on. In short, the abuse involves careful calculation over a period of time. Here is Hilary Eldridge describing one aspect of the process:

> When initially assessed, offenders usually engage in denial. They deny, minimize, excuse or justify their offending and blame others in much the same way as most human beings who are guilty of engaging in reprehensible behaviour.... In order to break through the excuses into reality, the assessor needs to know that what usually happens is that the offender thinks before he acts: imagines what he might do, and chooses or targets a child. Many offenders plan how to get the child to comply and prevent them disclosing, having first disempowered or manipulated people who might protect the child.... Sexual abuse of children is rarely incident based, it usually takes place within the context of relationships and involves the corruption of those relationships. (2000: 317)

Perhaps the most blatant examples of violence against women involving deliberate intention comes in the closely related areas of pimping and pornography. In both of these free market industries, men coordinate their activities to sexually, physically and economically exploit women and children. These industries are big business: Cole (1995: 47) reports that American men spend fifty million dollars a day on prostitution and, as noted earlier, in the United States there are more pornography outlets than McDonald's restaurants, generating $10 billion dollars a year (MacKinnon 1993b: 21). Like other industries, pimping and pornography respond to the globalization of labour and markets. One example of this is the influx of Eastern European women trapped in systems of prostitution in Western Europe since the fall of the Berlin Wall in 1989. Another example is so-called sex tourism in Southeast Asia in which Japanese, European and North American men travel to countries such as Thailand with the express purpose of sexually abusing Asian women and children. Women and children are commodified both by the pimps and pornographers and by their customers. Both the sellers and the buyers act out of choice (one does not "accidentally" make a pornographic film), which involves a series of decisions. And, as with the soldier-rapists, to the extent that they act out of choice they should be held accountable for the harm they do.

ACCOUNTABILITY

The most thorough exploration of the accountability of perpetrators of violence against women of which I am aware comes in Sharon Lamb's (1996) text *The Trouble with Blame: Victims, Perpetrators and Responsibility*. Centrally, Lamb maintains that all perpetrators have a will. This is true even of men who as children suffered "monumental abuse" by parents or institutions. Lamb calls this will "personified choice" (1996: 157). In spite of the excuses perpetrators use—outright denial, minimizing harm, blaming external forces such as childhood history, impulsivity, biology and cultural context—they in fact know what they are doing, as evidenced, for example, by the planning and foresight that goes into many men's sexual abuse of children.

In any process of violence there are three players: the victim, the perpetrator and society at large. As I suggested earlier, following Arendt, one of the effects of violent action is to make the world a more violent place. We are all affected by the perpetrator's actions. Though she does not use the terminology, Lamb suggests viewing men's sex/sexual violence as a practice of group-based discrimination in which crimes are committed not against individuals *per se*, but against an entire gender. This conceptualization conforms with lived experience in which the rights and freedoms of all women and girls are diminished by, for example, the threat of stranger rape. Lamb goes on to argue that women should have a special say in what social actions would be protective for them, what would be a fitting penance for crimes against women and "what kind of repayment is necessary to individuals and to women in general" (1996: 170). Though she does not mention them, victim impact statements used in some judicial procedures could be a step in the right direction, though they also need to be expanded to cover harm to women as a social category.

Turning now to the question of punishment, Lamb argues that state sanctioning fulfills a social purpose beyond the perpetrator/victim dyad. She writes:

> One of the strongest arguments for punishment emphasizes that it

has the ability to communicate something about social values in a broad and explicit way. In punishing a sexual offender or a man who batters his wife, we communicate to him, to ourselves, and to the community that what he did was wrong. Whether or not punishment changes actual perpetrator behaviour, this potential to communicate several broad messages reaches beyond the area of individual improvement.... Punishing also says to a sex offender that we want him to suffer the pain of remorse, and to repent. (1996: 167)

Just as the original crime affects three entities, so does punishment. The perpetrator is addressed directly, but so are the victim and society at large. Lamb argues:

> Punishment can communicate something important to the victim. Although it does not erase the crime nor the injury, it pronounces social opinion about her relative responsibility, proclaims that what happened to her was wrong, validates her rights, and thus allows her the luxury of not having to overstate her own rights and her own suffering. This is not to say that sex crimes are merely crimes against victims—they are also crimes against society. It is very important for society to begin to see itself as harmed by these crimes against women. And if rape, sexual abuse, and battering of women were to be considered fundamental crimes against society, we would find less ambiguity about punishing perpetrators. (1996: 169)

Finally, Lamb argues that the point of punishment should be reparation as embodying both repentance and reconnection with the community. The object becomes one of rehabilitation as the only way to forestall recidivism. This cannot be achieved if the offender is left alone with his thoughts. Instead, Lamb proposes that offenders be assigned to socially useful labour of a particular kind. Inasmuch as the crimes under consideration are crimes against women and children, reparation in the form of labour should be performed for organizations whose mandate is to support and advocate for these victims. In Lamb's words,

> But if prisoners were expected to work hard in ways that were useful to battered women's movements, to improving the lives of women and children (the very people whose lives they have harmed in a broad sense by their crimes against society), these men would reconnect not only to society and the hoped-for values of society, but also to the very people whom they have harmed. Such good work could at its best reinforce nonsexist values, provide education, and rebuild character. (1996: 175)

While intellectually satisfying, this proposal may not be practicable in reality. Most obviously, most transition houses and women's shelters must keep their addresses confidential to forestall batterers from stalking their ex-partners. More generally, how can a shelter claim to offer sanctuary/ refuge when men who are known to be violent toward women are out back mending the fence? Of course the battered women's movement encompasses more than just shelters and not all work is facility-based. Perhaps offenders could be put to use in fundraising drives.

CONCLUSION

If we are serious about the project of ending men's sex/sexual violence, we must begin where the violence begins—with the perpetrators themselves. We must challenge at every turn their attempts at diversions, including their victim blaming and their attempts to cast themselves as victims. Men are not so crippled by past experiences of oppression that they have no choice but to be violent. Writing on black men's experience of racism Amina Mama states:

> There has been a tendency, particularly with black discourse, to blame female abuse by black men on racism. It therefore needs to be said that however bad racial oppression may be, *racism does not take up the hand of the black man and oblige him to beat up his partner*. There are many different ways of responding to oppression. Female abuse is not racially or ethnically linked, but a function of gender inequality which prevails, whether one is considering marriage, co-habitation or visiting relationships. (2000: 54–55, emphasis added)

Men are socialized to be violent, particularly to be violent toward women and children. They are socialized to feel a sense of entitlement and thus to feel that, for example, sexual access to a woman is theirs by right. As boys, many men learn that size equates with dominance. But socialization does not completely abrogate individual choice. In spite of their socialization some men eschew violence. We need to know more about these men. We also need to establish principles of accountability that require men to face up to their responsibility and which speak to the victim, the perpetrator and society at large that their actions were wrong and that harming women is harming society at large. In part this may entail viewing men's sex/sexual violence as a form of group-based discrimination. Finally, recognizing that leaving a violent man in a cell alone with his thoughts will not bring about attitudinal change, we need to work out methods of reparation which embody both repentance and reconnection with the community. At best, such reparation could go directly to support the women and children who are victims of men's violence.

From the earliest days of the feminist anti-violence movement, there has been tension regarding state intervention. Historically, law has not protected women. While we have lobbied for changes, such as shifting the definition of rape to one of sexual assault, some feminists have worried that increasing the power of the state is not in women's interests. In the next chapter I will examine some examples of feminist interventions into the violence process which seek to invest agency in women.

NOTES

1. It should be noted the *Verstehen* can be translated as either understanding or empathy, and means both. Weber's project seems to have been to distinguish the former from the latter. Thus he separated *Verstehen* (interpretive understanding) from *nachfühlendes Verstehen* (empathic understanding) (Ringer 1997: 92 and 96).

2. Whether in practice incarceration in a secure hospital is experientially different from incarceration in prison may be moot.

3. Throughout Eastern Europe after the fall of communism and attendant rise of a "free press," pornography flooded in. MacKinnon quotes Yugoslav critic Bogan Tirnanic as saying the Yugoslav pornography market was "the freest in the world." This may be an exaggeration. However, it is the case that even mainstream news-type magazines carried pictures of naked women in poses of sexual display. MacKinnon goes so far as to claim: "When pornography is this normal, a whole population of men is primed to dehumanise women and to enjoy inflicting assault sexually" (1993a: 28). As in other examples, here MacKinnon may be overstating the case. As I argue elsewhere, the relationship between pornography and individual men's behaviour is not a lockstep cause and effect model MacKinnon seems to favour. For the purposes of this paragraph however, I accept MacKinnon's claim that pornography was freely available in the former Yugoslavia and its use was prevalent among soldiers and paramilitaries.

4. One may argue in mitigation that he was an inexperienced, doubtless scared, bravado-filled man-child without the courage or self-esteem to say no. Those factors do not absolve his culpability, though they should be weighed in the consideration of punishment.

7. FEMINIST INTERVENTIONS

INTRODUCTION

In the long term, the most effective interventions into men's sex/sexual violence occur before male sexual desire is constructed by the existing culture. This entails exposing and critiquing the hegemony of male supremacy and its prescribed gender relations. Crucially, we need male exemplars for boys, men who can model relations with women based on respect for women's full humanity. For this reason it is imperative that the lives of non-violent men, as seen through the prism of pro-feminism, be made available to boys as they struggle to understand what it means to be a man. This is a long-term strategy to be built upon by successive generations of men.

In the more immediate term, it is at the nexus of choice and accountability that intervention is possible. Beginning in the 1970s feminists lobbied governments to make violence against women visible and hence actionable under criminal law. Their successes are notable. To take just two examples, a model first developed in Duluth, Minnesota, required mandatory arrest for wife beaters. The second, in Canada, was the redefinition of rape in the Criminal Code to sexual assault. While both of these had significant impact on the treatment of individual victims of violence, as noted at the end of the previous chapter, many feminists worried that increasing the power of the state was not always in the interests of women. And so, new models were proposed to empower women while holding men to account for their actions. I will concentrate on three of these: civil actions against the producers and sellers of pornography; viewing pornography through the lens of human rights legislation; and "johns' school" for men who seek sex with street prostitutes.

MODEL ORDINANCE

The effort to hold pornographers to account for the harm they do to women and children was spearheaded in the United States by Andrea Dworkin and Catharine MacKinnon. They proposed a civic remedy, a municipal bylaw (in American terminology, an ordinance) under which women, men and children harmed by pornography could take legal action against the producers and sellers of pornography. Their definition of pornography is exhaustive:

The graphic sexually explicit subordination of women through pictures and/or words that also includes one or more of the following:

a) women are presented dehumanized as sexual objects, things, or commodities; or

b) women are presented as sexual objects who enjoy humiliation or pain; or

c) women are presented as sexual objects experiencing sexual pleasure in rape, incest, or other sexual assault; or

d) women are presented as sexual objects tied up or cut up or mutilated or bruised or physically hurt; or

e) women are presented in postures or positions of sexual submission, servility, or display; or

f) women's body parts—including but not limited to vaginas, breasts or buttocks—are exhibited such that women are reduced to those parts; or

g) women are presented being penetrated by objects or animals; or

h) women are presented in scenarios of degradation, humiliation, injury, torture, shown as filthy or inferior, bleeding, bruised or hurt in a context that makes these conditions sexual.

In this definition, the use of men, children, or transsexuals in the place of women is also pornography. (MacKinnon 1993b: 121–22, note 32)

The strength of this definition is that it outlines what pornography actually does. Unlike the (American) state's definition of obscenity as prurient interest in sex, this definition is not open to interpretation, though opponents tried to typify it as such. Also unlike the obscenity definition, this definition does not make reference to community standards. In short, the definition enumerates specific harms.

The most important thing to remember about the model ordinance is that it is a civil, not criminal law. Action under the ordinance is initiated not by state agents such as the police and public prosecutor, but rather by individual women who have been harmed one way or another by pornography. It casts pornography as a violation of the equality rights embedded in the Fourteenth Amendment to the U.S. Constitution. It describes pornography as a "systematic practice of exploitation and subordination which differentially harms women" (Minneapolis Ordinance in Dworkin and MacKinnon 1997: 427).

The model ordinance specifies four grounds by which those involved in the production and distribution of pornography may be held accountable in civil court. The first is discrimination by trafficking in pornography. This refers to the sale, exhibition or distribution of pornography.[1] The second is coercion into pornographic performances. Any person who is "coerced, intimidated, or fraudulently induced" into performing in pornography may sue the makers, sellers, distributors and exhibitors of pornography.[2] Third, anyone who has had pornography forced upon them in either a public or private space may take legal action against those responsible. And fourth, any person who is assaulted, physically attacked or injured in any way directly caused by a specific piece of pornography may take legal action against the immediate perpetrator himself but also the makers and sellers of pornography.

Hearings into whether the model ordinance should be adopted were held in Minneapolis, Indianapolis, Los Angeles and the state of Massachusetts. These hearings heard from a range of differently situated individuals. Some were academics such as Edward Donnerstein and Pauline Bart who provided expert opinion on the causal link between pornography and aggression. Some were women and gay men who testified as to how they had been personally harmed by pornography, either forced to perform in pornography and/or forced to view and re-enact pornographic scenarios. Testimony as to the constitutionality of the model ordinance was provided primarily by Catharine MacKinnon. Speaking against the proposed ordinance were civil libertarians and representatives of booksellers.

The first argument against the ordinance was that it creates a "chilling effect" on booksellers, who would have to vet each publication before displaying it. This is a specious argument. When, for example, jurisdictions require that pornography be kept out of sight of children, the booksellers have no problem determining which publications should go on the top shelf. Traditional or mainstream bookstores, which do not currently stock pornography, know which publications to avoid. The second argument is that for all its exhaustiveness, the definition in the ordinance of pornography is vague. Representatives of booksellers argued that "sexually explicit subordination of women graphically depicted" (the ordinance's basic definition of pornography) is difficult to identify. There is some validity in the notion that men look at the subordination of women and see sex— that, after all, is the point of pornography—but the eight dependent subclauses of the definition of pornography presented above should be sufficient to provide a guideline between pornography and erotica. More fundamentally, pornography makers and sellers are acutely aware of sexually explicit subordination of women because that *is* precisely what they make and sell.

The most difficult, and ultimately successful, challenge to the model ordinance concerns the First Amendment right to free speech. It would appear that to the original Founders of the U.S. Constitution the danger addressed in the First Amendment is that of a government seeking to suppress the broadcast of views critical to its functioning. In short, the purpose of the First Amendment was to guard from censorship the views of government critics. However, it appears to me that particularly in the latter half of the twentieth century, the principle of free speech has been idolized to the point of fetishism. Even when it is recognized that free speech may harm some others—for example racial invective leading to lynching—the mere fact that it is speech is sufficient to merit constitutional protection. Some legal scholars go so far as to claim that the more odious the speech the more it is in need of protection. Thus a march by the Nazi Party through a neighbourhood populated largely by Jews is granted First Amendment protection. The argument of feminists— that pornography is more than words and pictures but actual practices of subordination—was lost to the claim that pornography is speech and should be protected.

In an essay entitled "To Be and Be Seen: The Politics of Reality," feminist philosopher Marilyn Frye offers the following analogy:

> Imagine two people looking at a statue, one from the front, the other from the back, and imagine that the one in front thinks the one in back must be seeing exactly what he is seeing. He cannot fathom how the other can come up with a description so different from his own. It is as though women are assumed to be robots hooked up to the senses of men—not using senses of our own, not authoring perception, not having and generating a point of view. And they cannot fathom how we must be wired inside, that we could produce the output we produce from the input they assume to be identical with their own. The hypothesis that we are seeing from a different point of view, and hence simply seeing something he cannot see, is not available to a man, is not in his repertoire, so long as his total conception of the situation includes a conception of women as not authoritative perceivers like himself, that is, so long as he does not count women as men. And no wonder a man finds women incomprehensible. (1983: 165–66)

It would seem that this is the case for pornography—different people see it from different perspectives. Pornography apologists, civil libertarians and ultimately judges up to the U.S. Supreme Court looked at pornography and saw sex as expressive speech whereas feminists saw sex as repressive action. The perceptual gulf was too great and the ordinance ruled unconstitutional. An attempt was made to modify the ordinance but that too was struck down.

PORNOGRAPHY AND HUMAN RIGHTS

Susan Cole has taken Dworkin and MacKinnon's model and adapted it to fit the Canadian context in which citizens look to the state to protect rights and freedoms. Canadians are much less litigious than are Americans. Additionally, Canada has both federal and provincial bodies designed to adjudicate human rights violations. Such tribunals are at the heart of Cole's proposals.

Cole defines pornography as the "sexually explicit subordination of women and children in pictures and in words, produced for the sake of sexual gratification" (1995: 106). This is an improvement on the Criminal Code of Canada definition of obscenity as the undue exploitation of sex (cf. Criminal Code 159.8). In her definition Cole identifies the power relations in pornography and also identifies the purpose of pornography, namely sexual gratification for consumers. In short, Cole identifies the problem of pornography as not its explicitness but its acts of violence and degradation depicted as practices of sex. Focusing on subordination, Cole's definition allows us to view pornography as a violation of women's human rights.

Cole identifies three categories of women who are harmed by pornography and who, under her proposal, could launch a legal action against pornographers. The first is the women whose sexual violation is recorded in pornography. Any woman who was coerced or fraudulently induced to perform either in front of a camera or in front of an audience could take action against the manufacturers of pornography. The second group is women who have suffered physical attacks by men who consume pornography. They would be able to claim the pornographers were complicit in the attacks. Third, women who are confronted by pornography in their school or workplace or other public setting such as a variety store could file a claim of "intrusive display."

Cole identifies three advantages to adopting a human rights approach to pornography. First, it "reduces the dichotomy between public and private nurtured by obscenity and censorship law" (1995: 86). It recognizes, in other words, that women are often harmed by pornography in the privacy of their homes. Second, allowing women to sue for damages attacks the profit motive of pornography. It also puts money in the hands of women rather than the government (through fines). Third, it removes the state and its agents from the equation and in the process empowers women.

Since Cole proposed this human rights approach, a number of cases of pornography have been heard by the Ontario Human Rights Commission. Forcing women to look at pornography in the workplace has been construed as sexual harassment. Perhaps more significantly, in the case of *Regina vs. Butler* the Legal Education and Action Fund (LEAF—a feminist organization dedicated to promoting women's equality) successfully argued before the Supreme Court of Canada that materials that are degrading and dehumanizing to women should be deemed obscene. While these are significant gains, the old apparatus of obscenity and censorship laws remains in place and are differentially used against lesbian and gay materials.[3]

JOHNS' SCHOOL

The third example of feminist intervention I wish to address concerns men who seek sex from street prostitutes. So-called "johns' schools" have been established in various U.S. and Canadian jurisdictions but the program I am most familiar with is the Kerb-Crawler Re-Education Program, which operated in West Yorkshire, United Kingdom, from November 1998 to November 1999. The program was administered by the Research Centre on Violence, Abuse and Gender Relations, Leeds Metropolitan University,[4] working in conjunction with the West Yorkshire Police Authority.

The program offered a one-day school as a diversion from the court system for men who had been arrested for soliciting for prostitution. Men picked up by the police were given the option of attending the one-day school as an alternative to a court appearance, publicity and fine. In an effort to be self-financing, the program charged a fee of £110 to each attendee.

The major stated aim of the program was

> to shift the emphasis from the woman in prostitution to those who buy her. It recognizes street prostitution as an exploitation of women and also of children and a focus on kerb-crawlers as a means of creating safer communities. (Hanmer 2000b: 5)

To achieve this aim, the program had a number of components. Some were strictly factual, such as a police presentation on legislation related to kerb-crawling and a health worker's talk on sexually transmitted diseases. Other components were much more challenging for the men, such as the reality of prostitution from the perspective of the women and children and the role of pimps not just economically exploiting the women and children but also controlling them through threats and violence. In discussing the effects of the men's actions in buying sex, the program stressed that prostitution is not a victimless crime. Rather, it affects the women and children trapped in it, the local community and the family of the kerb-crawler. Additionally, the program presented a session on feminist analysis of violence against women and children and its relationship to masculinity. The day closed with a group interaction focusing on what brought the men to the program and an evaluation.

Judging from the men's self-reports, the program was successful in its broad purpose of re-education. They reported, for example, coming to see the women in prostitution as "real people" (Hanmer 2000b: 17), not just objects. This is a significant step, an awareness not achievable in the regular court process. Because the session on the realities of prostitution was a personal account, it had great impact. With regard to the session on the pimp dynamic (the tripartite relationship of the pimp, the prostitute and the john), also a personal account, some men reflected on it from their position as fathers of girls. In forcing them to question their past behaviour, all of the men said the program would help them stop re-offending. Some men went further, expressing an intention of "working at their personal relationships and beginning to respect women" (Hanmer 2000b: 18). Asked to comment on the general impact of the day, the men described feelings of guilt, shame, shock, humiliation, feelings of being bad and dirty. Together with the information and analysis of the program, these feelings may prevent re-offending.

Of course we must consider whether, in their self-reports, the men were simply parroting what the school instructors wanted them to say. I posed this question to the school director, Jalna Hanmer (2004: personal communication), and while she acknowledged that this probably happened, it is still true that the school had a beneficial effect. Among other things Hanmer points out that the evaluation form was open-ended such that the men chose their own words. Not all the men were particularly literate which might explain the broad language of feeling bad and dirty. While in the absence of follow up it is impossible to know what lasting effect the school had, Hanmer claims that at least some men came to recognize impacts (on themselves, on the women and children in prostitution, on their families and on the community at large) of their behaviour. Support for this comes in a paper given by Norma Hotaling, the founder of the first john school, in San Francisco. Hotaling states that of over 700 men who had attended the school, only three have been rearrested (1996: 14). Perhaps most important, Hanmer claims that unlike girls and women, boys and men generally receive little social education such that they are largely unaware of how their behaviour affects others. For some johns, at least, the school had the effect of helping them develop empathy.

Despite its effectiveness, the Kerb-Crawler Re-Education Program was discontinued after its pilot year. The underlying problem seems to have been an uneven response by the seven police divisions with street prostitution in West Yorkshire. By way of example, Huddersfield reported forty men for kerb-crawling whereas Milgarth reported only one (Hanmer 2000b, Table 1: 8). Overall, the relatively small number of men referred to the program, 139, indicates a lack of commitment to the program on the part of the police.

CONCLUSION

The most effective interventions occur prior to choice, prior to motivations, prior to desire as a socially constructed epiphenomenon. This entails exposing and critiquing the hegemony of male supremacy and its prescribed gender relations. Interventions involve radical root and branch change to the institutions and ideologies of our culture. One key area is the education of boys. Boys need an alternative vision of what it means to be a man, and an alternative vision of gender relations. Similarly, girls need to be educated to see themselves as other than receptacles of men's sex/sexual violence. To accomplish these radical goals, change is needed in all areas of culture: not only the formal education sector but also film, television, music videos and video games, to name just a few. Perhaps more fundamentally, both boys and girls need to be raised in an environment free from physical and sexual violence. They need to witness a growing gender equality in all areas of political, economic and social life.

Accomplishing these changes is the work of a lifetime for feminists and pro-feminist men. They may seem utopian but they *are* attainable goals. As various writers in this review have stated, men who abuse women and children must stop abusing and men who do not must stop supporting the men who do. At base, the problem is men. Accordingly, the solution must rest with men. Through theory, analysis and praxis, feminists can point the way but in the end, it is men who must walk the path.

NOTES

1. The section exempts public, university and college libraries in which pornography is available for study.
2. This section has a limitation of five years.
3. For a description of persecution of a gay bookstore by branches of the Canadian state, see Janine Fuller and Stuart Blackley (1995).
4. The Centre is now located at the University of Sunderland in the United Kingdom.

8. FEMINIST JURISPRUDENCE

INTRODUCTION

Before this literature review is completed some brief comment on the relationship of feminism to law is called for. It is a truism to state that the law is male in its structure, definitions, operations, personnel and products. Why should feminists have anything to do with it? One answer is summed up by MacKinnon:

> In point of fact, I would prefer not to have to spend all this energy getting the law to recognize wrongs to women as wrong. But it seems to be necessary to legitimize our injuries as injuries in order to delegitimize our victimization by them, without which it is difficult to move in more positive ways. The legal claim for sexual harassment made the events of sexual harassment illegitimate socially as well as legally for the first time. Let me know if you figure out a better way to do that. (1987: 104)

I know of no better way. As a major regulatory framework in many societies, the law has a central role to play in making situations of oppression visible and hence actionable both legally and socially. Accordingly, it is in women's interests to work for changes in the law. In addition to the example of sexual harassment which MacKinnon cites, one may point to equal pay, wife rape and the defence of provocation when women kill their abusive partners as cases in which feminist input into debates on law has brought about positive change. In this chapter I will consider first the metanarratives of various schools of feminist jurisprudence in domestic settings. I will then consider some applications of feminist approaches to law and the theory and practice of international law from the perspective of women.

DOMESTIC LEGAL THEORY

Carol Smart (1995) identifies three phases in the development of feminist jurisprudence. The first is represented by the phrase "law is sexist," the second by the phrase "law is male," and the third by "law is gendered" (1995: 187). The idea that law is sexist rests on a bedrock of equality-seeking liberal feminism. The focus of attention is how the law treats women and men differently. The male standard is retained, with a focus of bringing women up to that standard by, for example, developing gender-neutral language (spouse instead of wife, parent instead of mother). The goal of this program is the eradication of discrimination through the development of rights-bearing androgynous subjects. Accordingly, feminist legal activism in this phase focuses on issues such as pay equity and equality of opportunity. Its chief impact on laws related to violence concerned sexual harassment in the workplace as an equality issue. The drawback, however, is that if eradicating discrimination is dependent on the eradication of differentiation, "we have to be able to think of a culture without gender" (Smart 1995: 189).

The perspective that "law is male" is exemplified by writers such as Carol Gilligan (1982) and Catharine MacKinnon (1987). From their perspective, law is male both in its personnel (lawyers, judges and lawmakers) and in its values. MacKinnon in particular examines values such as objectivity and neutrality and finds them in fact to be masculine values masquerading as universalist ones. This is not to suggest that women are incapable of being objective or neutral, only that in doing so they, perhaps unconsciously, adopt a male point of view. These values exclude others such as caring, which are more in line with women's values. Smart criticizes this position as treating the law as a unity rather than problematizing it with its internal divisions. Additionally, it treats the male as unitary, risking thereby an appearance of biological determinism. Finally, divisions other than gender, such as race and class, are treated as "mere additions or afterthoughts" (Smart 1995: 190).

The most fully realized position, in Smart's view, is that of "law is gendered." This perspective focuses on the operation of law in not just reflecting gender but also creating it. It makes it possible to shed light on law's relationship with other cultural bodies such as the welfare state. In Smart's words,

> With this approach we can deconstruct law as gendered in its vision and practices, but we can also see how law operates as a technology of gender (de Lauretis 1987). That is to say we can begin to analyse law as a process of producing fixed gender identities rather than simply as the application of law to previously gendered subjects. (1995: 191)

Almost from its inception, the second wave of the women's liberation movement has struggled to expose the anti-woman nature of domestic law. Cole goes so far as to claim that in particular radical feminism is/was concerned with the everydayness of violence against women. She writes:

> It was the issue of violence against women that gave radical feminism its spark, and what distinguished radical feminism from its sister groups. By naming what happened to women, using terms that had not made their way into public consciousness, let alone

public policy, radical feminists tugged away at public awareness until the unspoken came out of its closet. We talked about rape, violence against women in the home, sexual harassment and more recently about incest. As activists and sociologists tried to make sense of the crisis, feminist research, the kind that listened to women, uncovered the truth that sexual abuse was epidemic, not occasional, more normal than marginal. (1995: 115–16)

In a review essay on legal responses to violence against women in Canada, Elizabeth Sheehy distinguishes *formal* equality from *substantive* equality. The former requires equality of treatment and that only to the extent that the men and women are similarly situated. Substantive equality looks beyond equating like with like toward an equality of outcomes. Of substantive equality Sheehy writes:

Are women and men in a given society equal recipients of the benefits and burdens of that society? Among women, are we equally credible when we speak in the justice system? Are we equally free of violent assault? Sometimes, the most productive route to substantive equality will be to use formal equality or equal treatment as a tool; at other times, the specific conditions of women's lives, including, for example, the threat and impact of male violence, or the racialized abuse experienced by African Canadian women, will require very particular rules or practices to move us toward equality. (1999: 62)

Formal equality leads to anomalous inequality as was the case of one trial Sheehy cites in which the lower court judges ruled that since men's beards and women's breasts are both secondary sex characteristics, and since it is not illegal to touch a man's beard, it cannot be illegal to touch a woman's breast (1999: 66). This literalization of gender neutrality led to a gender inequality by failing to recognize the social meanings of women's breasts in a climate of men's sex/sexual violence.

DOMESTIC LAW APPLICATIONS
Some of the early struggles to create a feminist jurisprudence focused on illuminating rape, wife battering and later child sexual abuse as issues of violence. These feminist legal activists lobbied ceaselessly for changes in the Criminal Code meant to encapsulate women's lived experience of violence as opposed to men's theory of harm. Here I will discuss just one such struggle, that of the legal perception of sexual assault.

In the late 1980s, I wrote a small book entitled *In Women's Interests: Feminist Activism and Institutional Change* (1988). In it I analysed the relationships between a grassroots feminist rape crisis centre and the various police detachments (municipal and RCMP) in its catchment area. With the formal backing of the Attorney-General's ministry, the rape crisis centre was successful in modifying police policy and procedures when dealing with victims of sexual assault. For example, after some negotiation, the police agreed a rape crisis worker could be present when the police interview a victim. Equally important, centre workers were given access to police training—both initial training for new recruits and ongoing training for line officers—in which they were able to dispel myths about rape (such as a prostitute cannot be raped) and more broadly could provide the officers with a feminist analysis of sexual assault based on the experiences of women victims. Another change was a formal agreement that the police would accept third party reports. These are anonymous reports of sexual assault which the police use for "intelligence" purposes. Though charges cannot be brought, they serve to apprise police of individual rapists—their practices and in some cases even their identities—and/or high risk areas. More generally, by having a designated police liaison worker, the centre was able to respond to and follow up when problems with police handling of sexual assault cases arose.

Another important area of feminist praxis on sexual violence is the ongoing lobbying for legislative change, to make the law in some way correspondent with women's lived experience. This work goes back to the earliest days of the modern women's liberation movement and continues on to the present. Here are some of the highlights of that effort:

1) In 1975–6 Section 142 of the Criminal Code was added as a first attempt at a so-called "rape shield" law. This section limited the extent to which defendants' lawyers could go on fishing expeditions into the complainant's sexual history.

2) In 1983 rape was legislatively redefined as sexual assault and the language employed was gender neutral. In effect, the reform collapsed gender-specific crimes of rape, indecent assault on a female and indecent assault on a male into one category, that of sexual assault. This definition was said to benefit victims by emphasizing the violence of the sexual assault. The prohibited behaviours were expanded beyond the old definition of rape as forced sexual intercourse to include unwanted sexual touching and the use of weapons and wounding. The new definition also removed the marital exemption, which previously had prohibited women from laying a charge of sexual assault against their husbands. Additionally, the requirement of recent complaint—that a victim report being assaulted at the earliest opportunity—was repealed. The rape shield was improved to deny the use of the complainant's history and the requirement that the victim's testimony be corroborated was abolished. Of these changes, Sheila McIntyre writes:

Proponents of the reforms hoped that by de-sexing the law's language and reclassifying it as a crime of violence, not an offence against public morals and not a matter of uncontrolled lust, the sexual double standards embedded in the law would disappear. (2000: 74–75)

3) In 1988 new sections of the Criminal Code related to sexual interference with a minor were added. These new offences—sexual interference, invitation to sexual touching and sexual exploitation—were written in gender neutral language, an acknowledgment that boys as well as girls can be the victims of men's sexual violence.

4) In 1992 Bill C-49 altered sections of the Criminal Code to provide the first positive definition of consent and yet another rape shield law. Drunk, drugged, coerced by threat or actual use of violence, or mentally unable to generate self-motivated behaviour all are situations in which women cannot give consent to sex. Accordingly, it is up to the man to seek out a positive expression of consent before pressing sexual activities. Silence alone does not indicate consent. In the case of children, they are said to be unable to formulate consent at all so regardless of what a child said, any sexual activity with the child is *ipso facto* statutory rape.

5) Finally, in 1997 Bill C-40 restricted the use of the complainant's medical and psychotherapeutic records.[1]

As I have presented it, the history of sexual assault law is a steady progression over thirty years bringing the law ever closer to women's lived experience. Of course it is not as simple as that. In particular, the numerous changes and refinements to the rape shield law were necessitated by *Charter* challenges. Of special note, the rape shield provisions were said to compromise the fair trial rights of the accused (Section 11.d of the *Charter*) and principles of fundamental justice (Section 7). To take just one example, in the case of *R. v. O'Connor*, a case which involved Bishop O'Connor, a Roman Catholic cleric and school principal accused of sexually assaulting young Aboriginal women, the defence successfully argued that the defendant should be given access to the complainant's counselling records. They claimed that such records would demonstrate that the complainant suffered from so called "False Memory Syndrome" and that her memories of abuse had been somehow planted in her by her feminist therapist. Rather than allow that to happen, the Crown dropped the charges against Bishop O'Connor. Thus we can see that for every progressive step in the legislation against sexual assault taken, there is a more or less successful backlash initiated by defence attorneys and ratified by the courts. The fundamental conflict between women's lived experience and men's view of male entitlement remains in force.

International Legal Theory

The textual products of international law—treaties, conventions, covenants and the like—and the institutions of international law must be exposed to critiques of male bias and improved to take account of the lived experience of half the world's population. Feminists have been at the forefront of doing this work.

To date most feminist work in international law has focused on human rights law. In a lengthy review article Karen Engle (1992) summarizes that work, identifying three trends in women's human rights advocacy. The first she describes as doctrinalist, which focuses on the analysis and interpretation of human rights texts. Engle characterizes them as liberal in their feminism and positivist in their approach to law. They see international human rights instruments as authoritative. Their object is to have those instruments recognized as applying to women.

The second trend is institutionalist. Engle views feminists associated with institutionalism as also liberal and positivist. They seem to accept international human rights law at face value and focus on the institutions which enact and enforce that body of law. They concentrate on two categories of institutions, mainstream bodies such as the Commission on Human Rights (CHR) and specialized bodies such as the Committee on the Elimination of Discrimination Against Women (CEDAW). The former, institutionalists claim, fail to give priority or indeed recognition to issues of human rights affecting women. The latter, which have women as their mandate, are derivative bodies and have not been granted the powers or resources necessary to bring about change. Institutionalists pay greatest attention to strategies aimed at increasing the enforcement of existing law rather than creating new law. These strategies include raising public awareness of the rights and freedoms nominally protected under international humanitarian law as it currently exists.

Engle's final trend has to do with external critique. Engle describes those who lead this trend as radical or cultural feminists. These feminists stand outside and critique the entire structure of international human rights as fundamentally male. They call into question every aspect of international human rights theory and practice and are the least optimistic about reform. Yet like their doctrinalist and institutionalist sisters, they maintain that feminists must remain active (though critical) participants in international human rights law.

Within the area of international humanitarian law there is a relative dearth of critical reflection. Most of the authors whose works figure prominently in this discussion simply assume that feminists can and should influence the development of international humanitarian law. They vary in their degree of relative optimism that the system can be reformed in women's interests but all take feminist activism as a given.

INTERNATIONAL LAW APPLICATIONS

International humanitarian law focuses on the interplay of two systems, a legal system and a war system. Catherine N. Niarchos (1995) argues that rape in war has been ignored because legal systems overlook women's pain and in a war system rape has been found to be an effective weapon. Both of these systems, she points out, are male dominated. She goes on to argue that "either by amendment or by declaration" (i.e., interpretation) international humanitarian law must be revised to reflect the concept of rape as extreme gender discrimination and as gynocide (as with femicide, the killing of women *qua* women). Niarchos also calls for a revised methodology for feminist jurisprudence, one which prioritizes individual experience and narrative. She writes:

> Feminist jurisprudence calls for a revised methodology: individual experience and narrative constitute the basis for argument; theory is recast based on experience and experience based on theory. The benefits of this methodology are twofold. First, through the inter-play of experience and theory, "the social dimension of individual experience and the individual dimension of social experience" are revealed. Second, when narrative is the basis of argument, reality and perception are more likely to coincide. Thus, in discussing rape the feminist approach requires an exposition of the facts in all their horrifying and indelicate detail. Only in this way can the full extent of female suffering be conveyed to a male-dominated legal culture. From this vantage point, it becomes apparent just how divorced from reality are legal protections for women in war. (1995: 654)

For Tamara Tompkins, the maleness of international humanitarian law is most fully exposed in its personnel. It is important to note that Tompkins' article appeared before the International Criminal Tribunal for the Former Yugoslavia had initiated trials. Accordingly, her comments are speculative. In the article she projects the danger of men speaking to each other at the tribunal about the wrongs inflicted on the international community through the mass rape of women. She worries that an injury to a woman will be transmogrified into one against the state. This looks, she writes, uncomfortably like "the international tribunal of men co-opting harm done to women for their own political and moral uses" (1995: 888). She further claims that the very real physical and psychological injuries suffered by women may be re-articulated into an abstract notion of a crime against humanity. In her words, "Against hu*man*ity? This is precisely the problem come full circle—rape is not a crime against hu*man*ity, it is a crime against a woman, and, by extension, all women" (1995: 889).

Tompkins' greatest fear is that in a perverse way rape in war will be confirmed as an injury between men. When the perpetrators, "victims" and judges all are men then this "unaccompanied by more, is punishing the crime on the perpetrators' terms" (1995: 889). Tompkins is not, however, without hope. She suggests that there may be a confluence of interests for the tribunal and for women, but only if women are allowed to speak in their authentic voices. She writes:

> As a forum for telling stories in the women's voices, expressing outrage on women's terms, and recording the horrors for the next posterity, the Yugoslavian war crimes tribunal holds out enormous possibilities. Women's advocates must, therefore, ensure that the stories get told inside the Tribunal and ensure that the unthinkable and unspeakable are thought and spoken about. They must then use the power of the media to tell the watching world what is being told to the Tribunal. This is where the goals of the Tribunal and the goals of women merge. (1995: 890)

From my perspective in 2004, Tompkin's analysis seems overly hopeful. There have been significant difficulties in prosecuting crimes against women in the International Criminal Tribunal for the Former Yugoslavia (ICTY) and its sister court, the International Criminal Tribunal for Rwanda (ICTR). During her tenure as Chief Prosecutor, Canadian judge Louise Arbour attempted to make prosecution of sexual assault charges a priority. To that end, she established a sexual assault committee to focus on cases of rape in the former Yugoslavia and in Rwanda. The strategy backfired partly because of the scale of the problem and the difficulty of marshalling evidence and partly because, paradoxically, the existence of the committee meant that other investigators such as those looking into possible cases of genocide came to think that "it isn't their job to pursue the rape cases" (Arbour in Off 2000: 338).

Arbour's attempts to highlight sexual assault cases was undermined by those in the Office of the Prosecutor below her. For example, Carol Off reports that the deputy prosecutor for Rwanda:

> dismissed sexual assault as very much a side issue for the prosecutor's office. "All that stuff about sexual harassment is for the politically correct people," said Muna, referring to the NGOs who pressured the tribunal to prosecute rape. Muna was much more interested in genocide. (2000: 337)

Thus the experience of the woman who had a piece of wood jammed into her vagina, leading to death, was dismissed as sexual harassment. This indicates a complete lack of understanding of the role of sexual crimes in genocide. Yet it is people like Muna who are running the tribunals.

Let me make a final comment on the difficulty of prosecuting sex crimes in the ICTY and ICTR. While both have a Victim Protection Unit, what is on offer is inadequate, providing protection only while the victim/witness is in the Hague or Arusha (the respective seats of the tribunals) or when traveling to and from them. Elenor Richter-Lyonette reports that a woman scheduled to testify in the case of Jean-Paul Akayesu was killed along with her family on January 5, 1997, in the Rwandan capitol of Kigali. She also claims a second woman has been killed since then (1998: 106).[2] Similarly, Stephanie Rousseau avers that at least two witnesses approached by ICTR investigators have been killed (1997: 8).

Against all this, I find myself more optimistic than Off, though not as wishful as Tompkins. Crimes of sexual violence *have* been successfully prosecuted at both tribunals. Particularly important are two findings in the case of Jean-Paul Akayesu, a Rwandan communal leader who was the first person ever to be charged with genocide. To begin with, the judges in that case developed a definition of rape as a crime of violence rather than a crime of honour, as it had been throughout the history of international humanitarian law. That conclusion was arrived at through four steps. First, the tribunal considered that "rape is a form of aggression" (Judgement, para. 687). Second, the judges pointed out that "the central elements of the crime of rape cannot be captured in a mechanical description of objects and body parts" (Judgement, para. 687). Third, the judges cited the Torture Convention as a useful model because it does not catalogue specific acts but rather focuses on the "conceptual framework of state-sanctioned violence" (Judgement, para. 687). Fourth, the tribunal enumerated the functions of rape:

> Like torture, rape is used for such purposes as intimidation, degradation, humiliation, discrimination, punishment, control or destruction of a person. Like torture, rape is a violation of personal dignity, and rape in fact constitutes torture when it is inflicted by or at the instigation of or with the consent or acquiescence of a public official or other person acting in an official capacity. (Judgement, para. 687)

Having set out how rape works in the context of conflict, the judges turned to defining the word itself:

> The Tribunal defines rape as a physical invasion of a sexual nature committed on a person under circumstances which are coercive. The Tribunal considers sexual violence, which includes rape, as any act of a sexual nature which is committed on a person under circumstances which are coercive. Sexual violence is not limited to physical invasion of the human body and may include acts which do

not involve penetration or even physical contact. (Judgement, para. 688)

In essence, the judges established three criteria: 1) the act was of a sexual nature; 2) the circumstances were coercive; and 3) the act was performed for some prohibited purpose such as intimidation.[3] Thus, there is no description of particular acts such as penetration. Additionally, acts such as forcing a teenaged girl to march naked before a crowd of villagers are seen as sexual violence.

Another important finding from the Akayesu trial is that rape was ruled a constituent act of genocide. In the judgement it was stated:

> [Rape and sexual violence] constitute genocide in the same way as any other act as long as they were committed with the specific intent to destroy, in whole or in part, a particular group targeted as such. Indeed, rape and sexual violence certainly constitute infliction of serious bodily and mental harm to the victim and are even, according to the Chamber, one of the worst ways of inflicting harm on the victim as he or she suffers both bodily and mental harm.... These rapes resulted in physical and psychological destruction of Tutsi women, their families and their communities. Sexual violence was an integral part of the process of destruction, specifically targeting Tutsi women and specifically contributing to their destruction and to the destruction of the Tutsi group as a whole. (Judgement, para. 731)

Two elements stand out in this paragraph. The first is that rape and sexual violence result in serious bodily and mental harm to the victim. This formulation is intentional and corresponds to Article 2(2)(b), one of the prohibited acts in the Genocide Article. In other words, the Court found that rape and sexual violence could be genocidal if committed with the requisite intent.

The second element of note is the recognition that the rape of a woman can affect her family and community. Adrien Wing and Sylke Merchán argue that rape can cause both women and men to withdraw from their societal roles. Keeping silent about what was done to them can require women to withdraw from familial and social roles as they attempt to deal alone with the consequences. Withdrawal may also be a reaction among fathers and husbands of rape victims or perceived victims. Not only has their family honour suffered, their masculine pride has taken a blow, for they have failed in their manly duty to protect "their" women. Whole communities can be affected by the rape of women. This can be particularly harmful to the community when women of the intelligentsia or other community leaders are targeted for rape, a pattern seen in both the former

Yugoslavia and Rwanda, including Taba commune, where Akayesu was the communal leader. On Bosnia Wing and Merchán write:

> The systematic rape of Muslim women in Bosnia could potentially result in the complete destruction of the Muslim social fabric. Because of the centrality of the concept of honour, the rape of one female member of the family can bring shame and disgrace to not only her immediate family, but also to the entire extended family. Thus, that family will not command the same position of respect in the community. This change in one family's social position will then affect the social ordering of the community, as another family may step into the vacuum left by the family of the rape victim. As a consequence, the systematic violation of Muslim women will destabilize the social ordering in Bosnia to the extent that the population will be fragmented and diminished, allowing for easy manipulation of the remaining inhabitants. (1993: 24)

So, the judges recognize both the harm done directly to the rape victim and recognize the damage done to the community through the rape of women. In the next paragraph, the Court seems surprisingly progressive in recognizing the intersection of gender, sexuality and ethnicity. The judges wrote:

> The rape of Tutsi women was systematic and was perpetrated against all Tutsi women and solely against them....[4] As part of the propaganda campaign geared to mobilizing the Hutu against the Tutsi, the Tutsi women were presented as sexual objects.... *This sexualized representation of ethnic identity* graphically illustrates that Tutsi women were subjected to sexual violence because they were Tutsi. Sexual violence was a step in the process of destruction of the Tutsi group—destruction of the spirit, of the will to live, and of life itself. (Judgement, para. 732, emphasis added)

What the judges are pointing to is intersectionality in which racism exacerbates sexism and sexism exacerbates racism. As I discussed in the chapter on intersectionality, this dynamic interaction generates violence as a complex fusion in which the two elements cannot be separated. Such violence may be of an intensity far in excess of the additive value of the two elements and, just as importantly, it may be qualitatively different from single-axis oppression or violence. Reflecting on feminist discussions of the eroticization of dominance and submission in an article on the former Yugoslavia, I have written:

> we may consider whether the perpetrator experiences his *national*

dominance as sexual and performs that national dominance by forcing [the victim] into a position of *sexual submission*. (2001: 215)

What the judges recognize is that the victims were raped not just as women and not just as Tutsi, but specifically as Tutsi women.

As well as linking gender, sexuality and ethnicity, we must underscore the long-term consequences of rape in armed conflict. In describing the psychological damage of sexual violence ("destruction of the spirit, of the will to live"), the judges recognized the enormous difficulty in rebuilding Rwandan society in the aftermath of widespread sexual violence. But perhaps what is most important about the judges' words is the simple recognition that rape in war is widespread and sometimes systematic, that it is not a random, isolated act. No more can rape in war be dismissed as the predictable and acceptable behaviour of a conquering army. No more can it be dismissed as the act of individual randy soldiers. The judges made clear that the rapes and sexual violence in Rwanda were sanctioned, coordinated and were part of a policy of genocide.

Julie Mertus reminds us, however, that "a war crimes tribunal is, after all, only a war crimes tribunal" (2000: 144). Having reviewed the Akayesu trial, we may ask more specifically and perhaps less cynically, is this a victory for women? First we might consider the time it took. Akayesu was indicted February 13, 1996. The trial began January 9, 1997, and the judgement was handed down September 2, 1998. Clearly, at this rate there will be relatively few trials before the tribunal is shut down. In this regard Mahmood Mamdani's account of South Africa's Truth and Reconciliation Commission may be instructive. According to Mamdani, the Commission identified only 20,000 South Africans to be victims of apartheid. That left the vast majority of citizens, millions of people, "in the proverbial cold" (2000: 178).

Let us consider the positives. The Rwandan Tribunal and the Yugoslav Tribunal are the first courts ever to try genocide. From 1948 to the 1990s genocide was merely a concept enshrined in a convention. Second, the fact that both tribunals are international, set up by and answerable to the United Nations, is important for there can be no charge of victor's justice as there was at Nuremberg and Tokyo after the Second World War. Looking at the Akayesu trial specifically, it was the first international body which defined rape as a crime of violence, not a violation of honour. That definition has since been used in at least one other trial, that of Delalic et al. before the ICTY. Crucially, the Akayesu trial was the first time rape was identified as a constituent act of genocide. In this there is a recognition of the intersection of gender hatred and ethnic hatred, a recognition that in genocidal rape it is not just one's gender identity that is violated but simultaneously one's ethnic identity, and that these are not separable.

Now let us examine the negative elements. Mertus argues that the punishment function of war crimes trials can "substantiate the suffering of victims, aiding the process of reclaiming an entitlement to subject-hood" (2000: 154). In Rwanda, as in other scenes of genocide, tens of thousands of raped and sexually mutilated women were murdered. For them there is no possibility of "subject-hood." Additionally, as suggested above, most living victims will not be asked to tell their stories. As in South Africa, only a small minority of victims will appear before the Tribunal and, through telling their story and seeing the guilty punished, be in some way restored to their former selves. But, realistically, the ICTR and ICTY are not concerned with individual victims. Their unstated mandate is to look at the "big picture," and direct their efforts at deterring future war criminals. They cannot prosecute every case of pillage, but if they successfully prosecute one, then precedent has been set and can be used in the future. In this sense the tribunals are primarily concerned with jurisprudence and the advancement of international humanitarian law. As well, representative prosecutions may even have a deterrent effect on future would-be war criminals. Given this practical/political reality, Kelly Dawn Askin has a suggestion: if trials are to be representative, let us ensure that they represent the range of crimes against women committed in wartime. Writing of the Yugoslav Tribunal, Askin suggests that: "At least one case of each and every pattern of sexual abuse must be prosecuted, i.e., rape, forced prostitution, genocidal rape, sexual mutilation, forced impregnation, forced maternity" (1997: 366).

CONCLUSION

To conclude this brief overview, all of the writers here considered take feminist activism within law as a given. The form such activism takes varies depending in part on the political orientation of the individual advocate and in part on the area of law under consideration. Concerning domestic law, the focus has been on revealing the maleness and/or structural gender of law. In relation to international humanitarian law, there is a consensus that activism is necessary most especially to ensure that women's authentic voices are heard.

Tracing the textual pathways of developing law is more than an academic exercise. Each step along such pathways has real consequences for real women on the ground. Indeed, one may go so far as to claim that the proof of feminist analysis is in the pudding of real women's actual experience. Accordingly, it is beholden upon feminist theorists to continue to work at the rockface of jurisprudence, always keeping in mind the real life consequences of the adjudication of men's sex/sexual violence to the women who are its victims. Guarding against both complacency and complicity is best accomplished by keeping the experiences of victims of violence at the forefront of one's mind. LEAF learned this the hard way. In intervening in a Supreme Court challenge of the rape shield law, LEAF hired a well-known male lawyer who prepared a sketchy brief including examples of possible infringements to the right of fair trial. No mention was made of the relationship of provisions in the Criminal Code and women's right to equality as enshrined in the *Charter of Rights*. Other feminists, particularly those engaged in seeking civil remedies for women harmed by pornography, were critical of LEAF's strategy, noting in particular the absence of equality arguments. LEAF learned from this experience and now holds consultative workshops throughout the country prior to formulating its activist agenda. The result is the LEAF today is more rather than less relevant to women's lives (for further details see Razack 1991).

Law does not in any absolute way prevent sexual violence. Experience in national jurisdictions demonstrates that most sexual assaults are not reported and of those that are, only a minority result in an arrest and trial. That all sexual offenders are not caught does not mean, however, that the law is of no value. One of the functions of law is the symbolic expression of a society's values. It makes a difference to women that prohibitions of sexual violence are codified. It may even make a difference to some men.

The same is true at the level of international jurisdiction. By its decision in the case of Jean-Paul Akayesu, the International Tribunal for Rwanda made war rape both visible and actionable under international humanitarian law. Many, perhaps most, perpetrators of sexual violence in Rwanda and the former Yugoslavia will not be prosecuted. But even one prosecution has symbolic value. It says to women everywhere that rape in war is not an accepted or acceptable inevitability. It says to men that they cannot act in war with complete impunity. It says to both women and men, especially those outside zones of conflict, that sexual violence in war is an issue about which we all should be concerned and on which we should be willing to act. Perhaps, even, in the next war some men, some commanders will be constrained in their behaviour. It is a start.

NOTES

1. The full text of sexual offences in the current Criminal Code is included in Appendix II.
2. Richter-Lyonette also reports that a male witness was killed just after he had picked up his travel money to get to Arusha. While it is impossible to know, it may be that in his case the motive was robbery (Richter-Lyonette, 2002, personal communication).
3. Assumedly, acts which meet the first two criteria but not the third would be prosecutable in a national court using the state's criminal code.
4. This is not entirely accurate. Moderate Hutu women, such as the government minister Mme Agathe Uwilingiyimana, were subject to sexual violation. In some cases, Hutu women married to Tutsi men were also raped. In Taba, at least one Hutu woman was beaten for refusing to divulge a Tutsi's hiding place but there is no evidence of a Hutu woman being raped in that commune.

Conclusion

Thirty-five years of feminist activism and research have produced a wealth of understandings on the meanings and consequences of men's sex/sexual violence. The conceptualizations presented in this book—especially those related to male supremacy, socially constructed gender and sexuality—constitute an analytical infrastructure, a framework in and by which specific instances of violence may be understood. Some areas remain under-theorized. We need to know much more about men who are not sexually violent and women who are. Intersectionality is an important preliminary model, but more analysis is needed to capture the complex dynamics among social statuses and their relation to violence. Crucially, we need to generate more sophisticated analyses of sex/sexual violence that is organized and centrally coordinated, as when sexual violation is used as a tactic of ethnic cleansing. These reservations notwithstanding, we have available today ways of perceiving and making sense of violence against women that we did not have thirty or even ten years ago. And with knowledge comes a force for change.

This text has investigated feminist analyses of violence against women. It found that they present such violence as unidirectional, discriminatory and always containing a sexual component whether overt or not. Accordingly, throughout this work I have written of *men's sex/sexual violence*. I then explored feminist discourses on the ideological and structural practices of male supremacy and their role in perpetuating men's sex/sexual violence. Within that exploration, oppression, social control and dominance were identified as central ideological functions of violence that affect all women in a society. The socially organized and organizing practices of gender and sexuality were analysed as resulting in an eroticization of dominance and submission such that violence is experienced as sex, and, too often, sex is experienced as violence. This led to a review of MacKinnon's critique of sex and sexuality. The eroticization of dominance and submission was investigated as operating in systems of hierarchy additional to gender. The concept of intersectionality was explicated and I proposed that hierarchies such as gender and race may be sexualized and further, that these eroticized hierarchies may interact synergistically so as to produce an exponential of violence. Sex/sexual violence was then analysed as being not an event but rather a socially embedded process. This led to a discussion of choice and accountability for perpetrators, which in turn led to a brief discussion of feminist interventions into the violence process. I concluded with an examination of feminist jurisprudence in both the domestic and international arenas.

There is nothing inherent in men that makes them violent. The propensity for violence is not genetic. Men learn to be violent and, as I have shown throughout this book, men learn particular ways in which it is socially and culturally legitimate to direct that violence against women. What is learned can be unlearned. Crucially, as it is men who teach boys to be violent, so it must be men who teach boys attitudes of respect toward themselves and respect and empathy toward girls and women. Gender is not reified, fixed. Precisely because it is socially learned it is mutable. It is possible to hold up a different version of who and what a man is. This is why the work of pro-feminist men is so important. While as feminists women can teach our real and metaphorical daughters to stand up for themselves, to refuse second class status, at the end of the day change will come when men learn to eschew violence. Recall Itzin's formulation: what is needed is for abusing men to stop abusing and for other men to stop supporting them. To do so will require a sea change. Every institution in society, from the smallest and most private to the largest and most public, is in need of root and branch reform, radical reform if that is not an oxymoron. Until that day comes feminists and pro-feminist men must rally behind services that support women and children who have suffered violence, must lobby for changes in the Criminal Code such that the law mirrors women's experience of men's sex/sexual violence and, most importantly, must speak out when gender violence happens in their community.

In this book I hope to have presented a picture of the state of feminist knowledge about men's violence against women and children. Of course it is incomplete, a flash photo of what is in fact a continuous spiral of knowledge development. In closing I wish to point to the lacunae of feminist discourse on violence.

Most feminist analysis is restricted to individualized sex/sexual violence. A certain conceptual opacity that can and should be lifted surrounds sexual violence that is organized and perpetrated by state actors. This could include, but surely is not restricted to, feminist interrogations of bodies such as the ICTY and ICTR and their treatment of rape as a war crime. The newly created International Criminal Court may also be a site of contestation.

Once again I am led to reflect on Arendt's words. As she says:

> Only the fearful imagination of those who have been aroused by such reports but have not actually been smitten in their own flesh, of those who are consequently free from the bestial, desperate terror ... can afford to keep thinking about horrors. (1979: 441)

Perhaps that is one of the contributions this book can make: to provide others with a means of thinking about horror and its aftermath, a partial antidote to despair and immobilizing rage.

The best feminist theorists ground their work in the experiences of women who live in a culture that hates them. This grounding involves first and foremost a willingness to listen to women, to identify with women and a commitment to understanding that no woman is free until we all are free. It also involves recognizing that the gulf between theory and practice must be crossed by praxis, the interaction of thought and action. In this sense feminists live out Marx's thesis that "the philosophers have only *interpreted* the world, in various ways; the point, however, is to *change* it" (Marx 1972). Feminists, in other words, have a personal stake in the liberation of women. I am drawn to recall a slogan first enunciated in the Paris Spring of 1968 and later appropriated by feminists in the 1970s: "C'est pour toi que tu fais la revolution!" (It is for yourself that you make the revolution.)

Carolyn Nordstrom and Antonius Robben ask the question, "When does empathy turn into identification?" (1995: 14). This is a dilemma faced by many female researchers of violence against women. Boundaries between self and other can get lost or at least become blurred. As a feminist with an analysis of the operation of male dominance and the links between gendered sexuality and violence I know that what differentiates me from the women whose accounts of war rape I study is little more than good fortune. Their pain, anger, bewilderment become mine as I realize that only a fluke of geography separates us. Surely this feeling would be much more acute for women researchers who study violence in their own community.

Self-reflexivity is a tricky thing. If we allow it, it can offer insights into what at first glance is incomprehensible. It can allow us to develop a sense of solidarity with the women whose experiences of violence we seek to understand. It can be a powerful antidote to the trend of pathologizing victims of violence. But it can also lead us to some uncomfortable self-truths.

As a woman, I identify first and most easily with the female victims of violence. When I read about a battered woman who tried to avoid being beaten by changing her behaviour I empathize. I imagine myself in her place doing the same thing. When a female victim of war rape says she cannot speak of what was done to her for fear of ostracism by her family and community, I understand her reticence. By understand I mean I can easily project myself into her situation and can imagine myself doing and feeling the same things.

On the surface, I have nothing in common with the perpetrators of war rape. On the surface, I do not share members' resources with them. They are violent. I am not and cannot imagine myself being so. They are men, a whole different territory from my experience as a woman. And yet, as I reflect on their experience, I cannot see it as other than human. In my individual being, I cannot imagine wanting to harm another sexually. But as a social being, I know that broad swaths of human behaviour are motivated by greed, anger and delusion. On that level I understand the humanity of the perpetrators. On that level my self-reflexivity makes me uncomfortable.

It is a discomfort with which, at least at this point, I am willing to live. It teaches me that the perpetrators of violent crimes against women are not other worldly devils but humans containing the capacity for redemption. It also teaches me that no matter what forces acted upon them—peer pressure, socialization, testosterone—these men acted out of choice and should be held accountable for their actions. Hardest of all it teaches me not to "other" these men, to dismiss them as incomprehensible. Finally, it encourages, even obliges me to engage in the hard work of understanding these men's actions from their point of view. This is what Max Weber termed *Verstehen* or interpretive understanding. For only with such understanding will we begin to know how to change men's anti-social destructive behaviours of which sexual predation is one. In short, the discomfort of self-reflexivity may contribute to a dialectic of knowledge development.

Finally and paradoxically, maintaining one's capacity to be horrified can be of use. I do not wish to become jaded about war rape or any other issue of violence against women. To do so would dehumanize both me and the women whose accounts I wish to understand. It is right to be shocked and horrified by the human capacity to do evil. As Beverly Allen writes: "And sometimes it is necessary to feel terrible in order to remain sane. Then you must act" (1996: 38).

Sorting out the definitions, origins, intersections and processes of men's sex/sexual violence is an Amazonian task. The issues are complex, their meanings at times obscure and their relationships opaque. As I write (July 2004), news of sexual killings of young girls by individual men in Canada, Belgium and the United Kingdom are still fresh. In this context, if understanding men's violence seems Amazonian, stopping that violence takes on the character of the endless labour of Sisyphus, though as Albert Camus admonishes, "one must imagine Sisyphus happy" (1955: 91). For activists and theorists alike, despair is a common consequence of the work we do. It is forestalled only by a willingness to continue to think and to struggle. The writers included in this review provide the means and the inspiration to do that.

Appendix I

Geneviéve Bergeron, twenty-one, was a second-year scholarship student in civil engineering.

Hélène Colgan, twenty-three, was in her final year of mechanical engineering and planned to take her master's degree.

Nathalie Croteau, twenty-three, was in her final year of mechanical engineering.

Barbara Daigneault, twenty-two, was in her final year of mechanical engineering and held a teaching assistantship.

Anne-Marie Edward, twenty-one, was a first-year student in chemical engineering.

Maud Haviernick, twenty-nine, was a second-year student in engineering materials, a branch of metallurgy, and a graduate in environmental design.

Barbara Maria Klucznik, thirty-one, was a second-year engineering student specializing in engineering materials.

Maryse Laganière, twenty-five, worked in the budget department of the Polytechnique.

Maryse Leclair, twenty-three, was a fourth-year student in engineering materials.

Anne-Marie Lemay, twenty-seven, was a fourth-year student in mechanical engineering.

Sonia Pelletier, twenty-eight, was to graduate the next day in mechanical engineering. She was awarded a degree posthumously.

Michèle Richard, twenty-three, was a second-year student in engineering materials.

Annie St-Arneault, twenty-three, was a mechanical engineering student.

Annie Turcotte, twenty-one, was a first-year student in engineering materials.

Appendix II

Selections from the 2003 Criminal Code Relating to Sexual Violence

150.1 (1) Consent no defence—When an accused is charged with an offence under section 151 or 152 or subsection 153(1), 160(3) or 173(2) or is charged with an offence under 271, 272 or 273 in respect of a complainant under the age of fourteen years, it is not a defence that the complainant consented to the activity that forms the subject-matter of the charge.

151. Sexual interference—Every person who, for a sexual purpose, touches, directly or indirectly, with a part of the body or with an object, any part of the body of a person under the age of fourteen years is guilty of an indictable offence and is liable to imprisonment for a term not exceeding ten years or is guilty of an offence punishable on summary conviction.

152. Invitation to sexual touching—Every person who, for a sexual purpose, invites, counsels or incites a person under the age of fourteen years to touch, directly or indirectly, with a part of the body or with an object, the body of any person, including the body of the person who invites, counsels or incites and the body of the person under the age of fourteen years, is guilty of an indictable offence and is liable to imprisonment for a term not exceeding ten years or is guilty of an offence punishable on summary conviction.

153.(1) Sexual exploitation—Every person who is in a position of trust or authority towards a young person or is a person with whom the young person is in a relationship of dependency and who

(a) for a sexual purpose, touches, directly or indirectly, with a part of the body or with an object, any part of the body of the young person, or

(b) for a sexual purpose, invites, counsels or incites a young person to touch, directly or indirectly, with a part of the body or with an object, the body of any person, including the body of the person who so invites, counsels or incites and the body of the young person,

is guilty of an indictable offence and liable to imprisonment for a term not exceeding five years or is guilty of an offence punishable on summary conviction.

153.(2) Definition of "young person"—In this section, "young person" means a person fourteen years of age or more but under the age of eighteen years.

153.1 (1) Sexual exploitation of person with disability—Every person who is in a position of trust or authority towards a person with a mental or physical disability or is a person with whom a person with a mental or physical disability is in a relationship of dependency and who, for a sexual purpose, counsels or incites that person to touch, without that person's consent, his or her own body, the body of the person who so counsels or incites, or the body of another person, directly or indirectly, with a part of the body or with an object, is guilty of

(a) an indictable offence and liable to imprisonment for a term not exceeding five years; or

(b) an offence punishable on summary conviction and liable to imprisonment for a term not exceeding eighteen months.

155. (1) Incest—Every one commits "incest" who, knowing that another person is by blood relationship his or her parent, child, brother, sister, grandparent or grandchild, as the case may be, has sexual intercourse with that person.

163. (1) Corrupting morals—Everyone commits an offence who

(a) makes, publishes, distributes, circulates, or has in his possession for the purpose of publication, distribution or circulation any obscene written matter, picture, phonograph record or other thing whatever; or

(b) makes, prints, distributes, sells or has in his possession for the purpose of publication, distribution or circulation a crime comic.

163. (8) Obscene publication—For the purposes of this Act, any publication a dominant characteristic of which is the undue exploitation of sex, or of sex and any one or more of the following subjects, namely, crime, horror, cruelty and violence, shall be deemed obscene.

163.1 (1) Definition of "child pornography"—In this section, "child pornography" means

(a) a photographic, film or other visual representation, whether or not it is made by electronic or mechanical means,

(i) that shows a person who is or is depicted as being under the age of eighteen years and is engaged in or is depicted as engaged in explicit sexual activity, or

(ii) the dominant characteristic of which is the depiction, for a sexual purpose, of a sexual organ or the anal region of a person under the age of eighteen years; or

(b) any written material or visual representation that advocates or counsels sexual activity with a person under the age of eighteen years that would be an offence under this Act.

163.1 (2) Making child pornography—Every person who makes, prints, publishes or possesses for the purposes of publication any child pornography is guilty of

(a) and indictable offence and liable to imprisonment for a term not exceeding ten years; or

(b) an offence punishable on summary conviction.

163.1 (3) Distribution etc. of child pornography—Every person who transmits, makes available, distributes, sells, imports, exports or possesses for the purpose of transmission, making available, distribution, sale or exportation of any child pornography is guilty of

(a) an indictable offence and liable to imprisonment for a term not exceeding ten years; or

(b) an offence punishable on summary conviction.

163.1 (4) Possession of child pornography—Every person who possesses any child pornography is guilty of

(a) an indictable offence and liable to imprisonment for a term not exceeding five years; or

(b) an offence punishable on summary conviction.

163.1 (4.1) Accessing child pornography—Every person who accesses any child pornography is guilty of

(a) an indictable offence and liable to imprisonment for a term not exceeding five years; or

(b) an offence punishable on summary conviction.

170. Parent or guardian procuring sexual activity—Every parent or guardian of a person under the age of eighteen years who procures that person for the purpose of engaging in any sexual activity prohibited by this Act with a person other than the parent or guardian is guilty of an indictable offence and liable to imprisonment for a term not exceeding five years, if the person procured for that purpose is under the age of fourteen years or to imprisonment for a term not exceeding two years if the person so procured is fourteen years of age or more but under the age of eighteen years.

171. Householder permitting sexual activity—Every owner, occupier or manager of premises or other person who has control of premises or assists in the management or control of premises who knowingly permits a person under the age of eighteen years to resort to or to be in or on the premises for the purpose of engaging in any sexual activity prohibited by this Act is guilty of an indictable offence and is liable to imprisonment for a term not exceeding five years if the person in question is under the age of fourteen years or to imprisonment for a term not exceeding two years if the person in question is fourteen years of age or more but under the age of eighteen years.

271. (1) Sexual assault—Everyone who commits a sexual assault is guilty of
(a) an indictable offence and is liable to imprisonment for a term not exceeding ten years; or
(b) an offence punishable on summary conviction and liable to imprisonment for a term not exceeding eighteen months.

272. (1) Sexual assault with a weapon, threats to a third party or causing bodily harm—Every person commits an offence who, in committing a sexual assault
(a) carries, uses or threatens to use a weapon or an imitation of a weapon;
(b) threatens to cause bodily harm to a person other than the complainant;
(c) causes bodily harm to the complainant; or
(d) is party to the offence with another person.

273. (1) Aggravated sexual assault—Every one commits an aggravated sexual assault who, in committing a sexual assault, maims, disfigures or endangers the life of the complainant.

273. (2) Aggravated sexual assault—Every person who commits an aggravated sexual assault is guilty of an indictable offence and liable
(a) where a firearm is used in the commission of the offence, to imprisonment for life and to a minimum punishment of imprisonment for a term of four years; and
(b) in any other case, to imprisonment for life.

273.1 (1) Meaning of "consent" —Subject to subsection (2) and subsection 265 (3) "consent" means, for the purposes of sections 271, 272 and 273, the voluntary agreement of the complainant to engage in the sexual activity in question.

273.1 (2) Where no consent obtained—No consent is obtained, for the purposes of section 271, 272 and 273 where
(a) the agreement is expressed by the words or conduct of a person other than the complainant;
(b) the complainant is incapable of consenting to the activity;
(c) the accused induces the complainant to engage in the activity by abusing a position of trust, power or authority;

(d) the complainant expresses, by words or conduct, a lack of agreement to engage in the activity; or

(e) the complainant, having consented to engage in sexual activity, expresses, by words or conduct, a lack of agreement to continue to engage in the activity.

273.2 Where belief in consent not a defence—It is not a defence to a charge under section 271, 272 or 273 that the accused believed that the complainant consented to the activity that forms the subject-matter of the charge, where

(a) the accused's belief arose from the accused's

(i) self-induced intoxication, or

(ii) recklessness or willful blindness; or

(b) the accused did not take reasonable steps, in the circumstances known to the accused at the time, to ascertain that the complainant was consenting.

275. Rules respecting recent complaint abrogated—The rules relating to evidence of recent complaint are hereby abrogated with respect to offences under sections 151, 152, 153, 153.1, 155 or 159, subsections 160(2) and (3) and sections 170, 171, 172 and 173.

176. (1) Evidence of complainant's sexual activity—In proceedings in respect of an offence under sections 151, 152, 153, 153.1, 155 or 159, subsection 160(2) or (3) or section 170, 171, 172, 173, 271, 272 or 273, evidence that the complainant has engaged in sexual activity, whether with the accused or with any other person, is not admissible to support an inference that, by reason of the sexual nature of that activity, the complainant

(a) is more likely to have consented to the sexual activity that forms the subject-matter of the charge; or

(b) is less worthy of belief.

(2) Idem—In proceedings in respect of an offence referred to in subsection (1), no evidence shall be adduced by or on behalf of the accused that the complainant has engaged in sexual activity other than the sexual activity that forms the subject-matter of the charge, whether with the accused or with another person, unless the judge, provincial court judge or justice determines, in accordance with the procedures set out in sections 276.1 and 276.2 that the evidence

(a) is of specific instances of sexual activity;

(b) is relevant to an issue at trial; and

(c) has significant probative value that is not substantially outweighed by the danger of prejudice to the proper administration of justice.

(3) Factors that judge must consider—In determining whether evidence is admissible under subsection (2), the judge, provincial court judge or justice shall take into account

(a) the interests of justice, including the right of the accused to make a full answer and defence;

(b) society's interest in encouraging the reporting of sexual assault offences;

(c) whether there is a reasonable prospect that the evidence will assist in arriving at a just determination in the case;

(d) the need to remove from the fact-finding process any discriminatory belief or bias;

(e) the risk that the evidence may unduly arouse sentiments of prejudice, sympathy or hostility in the jury;

(f) the potential prejudice to the complainant's personal dignity and right of privacy;

(g) the right of the complainant and of every individual to personal security and to the full protection and benefit of the law; and

(h) any other factor that the judge, provincial court judge or justice considers relevant.

BIBLIOGRAPHY

Agger, Inger. 1994. *The Blue Room: Trauma and Testimony among Refugee Women: A Psycho-Social Exploration*. London: Zed Books.

Allen, Beverly. 1996. *Rape Warfare: The Hidden Genocide in Bosnia-Herzegovina and Croatia*. Minneapolis: University of Minnesota Press.

Allen, Sheila. 1994. "Race, Ethnicity and Nationality: Some Questions of Identity." In Haleh Afshar and Mary Maynard (eds.), *The Dynamics of 'Race' and Gender: Some Feminist Interventions*. London: Taylor and Francis, 85–105.

Arendt, Hannah. 1964. *Eichmann in Jerusalem: A Report on the Banality of Evil*. New York: Penguin Books.

_____. 1970. *On Violence*. New York: Harcourt, Brace and World.

_____. 1979. *The Origins of Totalitarianism*. New York: Harcourt Brace Jovanovich.

Askin, Kelly Dawn. 1997. *War Crimes Against Women: Prosecution in International War Crimes Tribunals*. The Hague: Klewer Law International.

Atmore, Chris. 1999. "Victims, Backlash, and Radical Feminist Theory: or The Morning After They Stole Feminism's Fire." In Sharon Lamb (ed.), *New Versions of Victims: Feminists Struggle with the Concept*. New York: New York University Press, 183–211.

Barnsley, Jan, and Pamela Sleeth. 1989. *Recollecting Our Lives: Women's Experience of Childhood Sexual Abuse*. Vancouver: Press Gang Publishers.

Barry, Kathleen. 1979. *Female Sexual Slavery*. New York: New York University Press.

_____. 1985. "Social Etiology of Crimes Against Women." *Victimology: An International Journal* 10, 1–4, 164–73.

Bart, Pauline B., and Patricia H. O'Brien. 1985. *Stopping Rape: Successful Survival Strategies*. New York: Pergamon Press.

Bhavnani, Kum-Kum. 1993. "Talking Racism and the Editing of Women's Studies." In Diane Richardson and Victoria Robinson (eds.), *Introducing Women's Studies: Feminist Theory and Practice*. London: MacMillan, 27–48.

Blatchford, Christie. 2004. "Heart of Darkness." *Globe and Mail*, June 18, A1.

Bok, Sissela. 1991. *Alva Myrdal: A Daughter's Memoir*. Reading, MA: Addison-Wesley.

Bourke, Joanna. 1999. *An Intimate History of Killing: Face-To-Face Killing in Twentieth-Century Warfare*. London: Granta.

Boyle, Karen. 2000. "The Pornography Debates: Beyond Cause and Effect." *Women's Studies International Forum* 23, 2, 187–95.

Boyle, Karen. 2004. *Media and Violence: Gendering the Debates*. London: Sage Publications.

Brownmiller, Susan. 1975. *Against Our Will: Men, Women and Rape*. Harmondsworth: Penguin Books.

Butler, Judith. 1997. *Excitable Speech: The Politics of the Performative*. New York: Routledge.

Cameron, Deborah. 1999. "Rosemary West: Motives and Meanings." *Journal of Sexual Aggression* 4, 2, 68–80.

Cameron, Deborah, and Elizabeth Frazer. 1987. *The Lust to Kill: A Feminist Investi-*

gation of Sexual Murder. Cambridge: Polity Press.

Camus, Albert. 1955. *The Myth of Sisyphus and Other Essays*. New York: Vintage Books.

Caputi, Jane. 1992. "Advertising Femicide: Lethal Violence Against Women in Pornography and Gorenography." In Jill Radford and Diana E. Russell (eds.), *Femicide: The Politics of Woman Killing*. Buckingham: Open University Press, 203–21.

_____. 1993. "The Sexual Politics of Murder." In Pauline B. Bart and Eileen Geil Moran (eds.) *Violence Against Women: The Bloody Footprints*. Newbury Park: Sage Publications, 5–25.

Caputi, Jane, and Diana E.H. Russell. 1992. "Femicide: Sexist Terrorism Against Women." In Jane Caputi, and Diana E.H. Russell (eds.), *Femicide: The Politics of Woman Killing*. Buckingham: Open University Press, 13–21.

Card, Claudia. 1991. "Rape as a Terrorist Institution." In R.G. Frey and Christopher W.Morris (eds.), *Violence, Terrorism and Justice*. Cambridge: Cambridge University Press, 296–319.

Clark, Lorenne M.G., and Debra J. Lewis. 1977. *Rape: The Price of Coercive Sexuality*. Toronto: Women's Press.

Cleaver, Eldridge. 1969. *Soul on Ice*. London: Jonathan Cape.

Cole, Susan G. 1989. *Pornography and the Sex Crisis*. Toronto: Amanita Press.

_____. 1995. *Power Surge: Sex, Violence and Pornography*. Toronto: Second Story Press.

Collins, Patricia Hill. 1993. "The Sexual Politics of Black Womanhood." In Pauline B. Bart and Eileen Geil Moran (eds.), *Violence Against Women: The Bloody Footprints*. Newbury Park: Sage Publications, 85–104.

Commission of Experts. 1994. *Final report of the commission of experts established pursuant to Security Council Resolution 780* (1992), submitted 27 May 1994. UNDOC S/1994/674 [On-line]. Available: http://www.igc.apc.org/tribunal.

Cornell, Druscilla (ed.). 2000. *Feminism and Pornography*. Oxford: Oxford University Press.

Crenshaw, Kimberlé. 1989. "Demarginalizing the Intersection of Race and Sex: A Black Feminist Critique of Antidiscrimination Doctrine, Feminist Theory and Antiracist Politics." *University of Chicago Legal Forum* 139, 139–67.

_____. 1995. "Mapping the Margins: Intersectionality, Identity Politics, and Violence Against Women." In Dan Danielsen and Karen Engle (eds.), *After Identity: A Reader in Law and Culture*. New York: Routledge, 332–54.

Danica, Elly. 1988. *Don't: A Woman's Word*. Charlottetown: Gynergy Books.

de Lauretis, Teresa. 1987. *Technologies of Gender*. Bloomington: Indiana University Press.

Dobash, R. Emerson, and Russell R. Dobash. 1979. *Violence Against Wives: A Case Against Patriarchy*. London: Open Books.

Dobash, Russell R., R. Emerson Dobash, Kate Cavanagh, and Ruth Lewis. 2000. "Confronting Violent Men." In Jalna Hanmer, Catherine Itzin (eds.), with Sheila Quaid and Debra Wigglesworth, *Home Truths About Domestic Violence: Feminist Influences on Policy and Practice, A Reader*. London: Routledge, 289–309.

Dworkin, Andrea. 1981. *Pornography: Men Possessing Women*. London: Women's Press.

_____. 1991. "Terror, Torture, and Resistance." *Canadian Women's Studies/Les Cahiers de la Femme* 12, 1, 37–42.

Dworkin, Andrea, and MacKinnon, Catharine. 1993. "Questions and Answers." In

Diana E.H. Russell, ed. *Making Violence Sexy: Feminist Views on Pornography.* Buckingham, U.K.: Open University Press, pp. 78–96.

Edwards, Anne. 1987. "Male Violence in Feminist Theory: An Analysis of the Changing Conceptions of Sex/Gender Violence and Male Dominance." In Jalna Hanmer and Mary Maynard (eds.), *Women, Violence and Social Control.* London: MacMillan Press, 13–29.

Eldridge, Hilary. 2000. "Patterns of Sex Offending and Strategies for Effective Assessment and Intervention." In Catherine Itzin (ed.), *Home Truths About Child Sexual Abuse: Influencing Policy and Practice, A Reader.* London: Routledge, 313–34.

Engle, Karen. 1992. "International Human Rights and Feminism: When Discourses Meet." *Michigan Journal of International Law* 13, 3, 517–610.

Enloe, Cynthia. 1989. *Bananas, Beaches and Bases: Making Feminist Sense of International Politics.* London: Pandora.

Fanon, Frantz. 1967. *The Wretched of the Earth.* Harmondsworth: Penguin Books.

Ferguson, Kathy E. 1984. *The Feminist Case Against Bureaucracy.* Philadelphia: Temple University Press.

Frye, Marilyn. 1983. *The Politics of Reality: Essays in Feminist Theory.* Freedom, CA: Crossing Press.

Fuller, Janine, and Stuart Blackley. 1995. *Restricted Entry: Censorship on Trial.* Vancouver: Press Gang Publishers.

Gavey, Nicola. 1999. "'I Wasn't Raped, but...' Revisiting Definitional Problems in Sexual Victimization." In Sharon Lamb (ed.), *New Versions of Victims: Feminists Struggle with the Concept.* New York: New York University Press, 57–81.

Gilligan, Carol. 1982. *In a Different Voice.* London: Harvard University Press.

Griffin, Susan. 1978. "Rape: The All-American Crime." In Mary Vetterling et al. (eds.), *Feminism and Philosophy.* Totowa: Littlefield, Adams and Co., 313–32.

Hague, Euan. 1997. "Rape, Power and Masculinity: The Construction of Gender and National Identities in the War in Bosnia-Herzegovina." In Ronit Lentin (ed.), *Gender and Catastrophe.* London: Zed Books, 50–63.

Hanmer, Jalna. 1978. "Violence and the Social Control of Women." In Gary Littlejohn et al. (eds.), *Power and the State.* London: Croom Helm. 217–38.

_____. 2000a. "Domestic Violence and Gender Relations: Contexts and Connections." In Jalna Hanmer and Catherine Itzin (eds.), *Home Truths About Domestic Violence: Feminist Influences on Policy and Practice, A Reader.* London: Routledge, 9–23.

_____. 2000b. *Report: Kerb-Crawler Re-Education Programme for the West Yorkshire Police Authority.* Leeds: Research Centre on Violence, Abuse and Gender Relations.

Hanmer, Jalna, Jill Radford and Elizabeth A. Stanko. 1989a. "Policing Men's Violence: An Introduction." In Jalna Hanmer, Jill Radford and Elizabeth A. Stanko (eds.), *Women, Policing, and Male Violence: International Perspectives.* London: Routledge, 1–12.

_____. 1989b. "Improving Policing for Women: The Way Forward." In Jalna Hanmer, Jill Radford and Elizabeth A. Stanko (eds.), *Women, Policing, and Male Violence: International Perspectives.* London: Routledge, 185–201.

Hearn, Jeff. 1998. *The Violences of Men: How Men Talk About and How Agencies Respond to Men's Violence to Women.* London: Sage.

Helliwell, Christine. 2000. "'It's Only a Penis': Rape, Feminism and Difference."

Signs: Journal of Women in Culture and Society 25, 3, 789–816.

Herman, Judith Lewis, with Lisa Hirschman. 1981. *Father-Daughter Incest*. Cambridge: Harvard University Press.

Hollway, Wendy. 1981. "'I Just Wanted to Kill a Woman' Why? The Ripper and Male Sexuality." *Feminist Review* 9 (October), 33–40.

hooks, bell. 1995. *Killing Rage: Ending Racism*. New York: Henry Holt Co.

Hotaling, Norma. 1996. "Women and Prostitution." Paper presented at the Violence, Abuse and Women's Citizenship Conference, November, Brighton.

Human Rights Watch. 1993. *War Crimes in Bosnia-Herzegovina, Vol. II*. New York: Human Rights Watch.

International Criminal Tribunal for Rwanda. Case No.: ICTR-96-4-T The Prosecutor Versus Jean-Paul Akayesu, Judgement. Accessed on ICTR site: http://www.ictr.org.

Itzin, Catherine. 2000a. "Child Sexual Abuse and the Radical Feminist Endeavour: An Overview." In Catherine Itzin (ed.), *Home Truths About Child Sexual Abuse: Influencing Policy and Practice, A Reader*. London: Routledge, 1–24.

_____. 2000b. "Child Protection and Child Sexual Abuse Prevention: Influencing Policy and Practice." In Catherine Itzin (ed.), *Home Truths About Child Sexual Abuse: Influencing Policy and Practice, A Reader*. London: Routledge, 405–45.

_____. 2000c. "Gendering Domestic Violence: The Influence of Feminism on Policy and Practice." In Jalna Hanmer and Catherine Itzin (eds.), *Home Truths About Domestic Violence: Feminist Influences on Policy and Practice, A Reader*. London: Routledge, 356–80.

Johnson, Sonia. 1987. *Telling the Truth*. Freedom, CA: Crossing Press.

Jones, Ann. 1994. *Next Time She'll Be Dead: Battering and How to Stop It*. Boston: Beacon Press.

Kaufman, Michael. 1997. "The Construction of Masculinity and the Triad of Men's Violence." In Laura O'Toole and Jessica R.Sciffmen (eds.), *Gender Violence: Interdisciplinary Perspectives*. New York: New York University Press, 30–51.

Kelly, Liz. 1988. *Surviving Sexual Violence*. Cambridge: Polity Press.

_____. 2000. "Wars Against Women: Sexual Violence, Sexual Politics and the Militarised State." In Susie Jacobs, Ruth Jacobson and Jennifer Marchbank (eds.), *States of Conflict: Gender, Violence and Resistance*. London: Zed Books, 45–65.

Kelly, Liz, Linda Regan and Sheila Burton. 2000. "Sexual Exploitation: A New Discovery or One Part of the Continuum of Sexual Abuse in Childhood?" In Catherine Itzin (ed.), *Home Truths About Child Sexual Abuse: Influencing Policy and Practice, A Reader*. London: Routledge, 70–86.

Kimmel, Michael S. 1990. "Clarence, William, Iron Mike, Tailhook, Senator Packwood, Spur Posses, Magic ... And Us." In Emilie Buchwald, Pamela R. Fletcher and Martha Roth (eds.), *Transforming a Rape Culture*. Minneapolis: Milkweed, 119–38.

Klein, Dorrie. 1981. "Violence Against Women: Some Considerations Regarding Its Causes and Its Elimination." *Crime and Delinquency* 27, 1 (January), 64–80.

Korac, Maja. 1996. "Understanding Ethnic-National Identity and Its Meaning: Questions From Women's Experience." *Women's Studies International Forum* 19, 1/2, 133–43.

Lamb, Sharon. 1996. *The Trouble with Blame: Victims, Perpetrators and Responsibility*. Cambridge: Harvard University Press.

MacKinnon, Catharine A. 1987. *Feminism Unmodified: Discourses on Life and Law.* Cambridge, Harvard University Press.

_____. 1989. *Toward a Feminist Theory of the State.* Cambridge: Harvard University Press.

_____. 1993a. "Turning Rape into Pornography: Postmodern Genocide." *Ms Magazine* July/August, 24–30.

_____. 1993b. *Only Words.* Cambridge: Harvard University Press.

_____. 1996. "From Practice to Theory, or What is a White Woman Anyway?" In Diane Bell and Renate Klein (eds.), *Radically Speaking: Feminism Reclaimed.* London: Zed Books, 45–54.

_____. 2003. *Sex Equality: Lesbian and Gay Rights.* New York: Foundation Press.

MacKinnon, Catharine A., and Andrea Dworkin (eds.). 1997. *In Harm's Way: The Pornography Civil Rights Hearings.* Cambridge: Harvard University Press.

MacLeod, Mary, and Esther Saraga. 1988. "Challenging the Orthodoxy: Toward a Feminist Theory and Practice." *Feminist Review* 28 (January), 16–55.

Mama, Amina. 2000. "Violence Against Black Women in the Home." In Jalna Hanmer and Catherine Itzin (eds.), *Home Truths About Domestic Violence: Feminist Influences on Policy and Practice, A Reader.* London: Routledge, 44–56.

Mamdani, Mahmood. 2000. "The Truth According to the TRC." In Ifi Amadimume and Abdullahi An-Na'Im (eds.), *The Politics of Memory: Truth, Healing and Social Justice.* London: Zed Books, 176–83.

Marchiano, Linda, with Mike McGrady. 1981. *Ordeal.* New York: Berkley Books.

Marx, Karl. 1972. "Theses on Feuerbach." In Robert C. Tucker (ed.), *The Marx-Engels Reader.* New York: W.W. Norton, 107–09.

May, Larry, and Robert Strikwerda. 1994. "Men in Groups: Collective Responsibility for Rape." *Hypatia* 9, 2 (Spring), 134–51.

McIntyre, Sheila. 2000. "Tracking and Resisting Backlash Against Equality Gains in Sexual Offence Law." *Canadian Women's Studies/Les Cahiers de la Femmes* 20, 3 (fall), 72–81.

Mertus, Julie. 2000. "Truth in a Box: The Limits of Justice Through Judicial Mechanisms." In Ifi Amadimume and Abdullahi An-Na'Im (eds.), *The Politics of Memory: Truth, Healing and Social Justice.* London: Zed Books, 142–83.

Mrsevic, Zorica, and Donna M. Hughes. 1997. "Violence Against Women in Belgrade, Serbia: SOS Hotline 1990–1993." *Violence Against Women* 3, 2, 101–28.

Niarchos, Catherine N. 1995. "Women, War and Rape: Challenges Facing the International Tribunal for the Former Yugoslavia." *Human Rights Quarterly* 17, 649–90.

Nordstrom, Caroline and Antonius C.G.M. Robben. 1995. "The Anthropology and Ethnography of Violence and Sociopolitical Conflict." In Caroline Nordstrom and Antonius C.G.M. Robben (eds.), *Fieldwork Under Fire: Contemporary Studies of Violence and Survival.* Berkeley: University of California Press, 14–24.

Off, Carol. 2000. *The Lion, the Fox and the Eagle: A Story of Generals and Justice in Rwanda and Yugoslavia.* Toronto: Random House Canada.

Price, Lisa S. 1988. *In Women's Interests: Feminist Activism and Institutional Change.* Vancouver: Women's Research Centre.

_____. 1989. *Patterns of Violence in the Lives of Girls and Women: A Reading Guide.* Vancouver: Women's Research Centre.

_____. 2001. "Finding the Man in the Soldier-Rapist: Some Reflections on Comprehension and Accountability." *Women's Studies International Forum* 24, 2,

211–27.

Radford, Jill. 1987. "Policing Male Violence —Policing Women." In Jalna Hanmer and Mary Maynard (eds.), *Women, Violence and Social Control*. London: MacMillan, 30–45.

———. 1992. "Introduction." In Jill Radford and Diana E.H. Russell (eds.), *Femicide: The Politics of Woman Killing*. Buckingham: Open University Press, 3–12.

Razack, Sherene. 1991. *Canadian Feminism and the Law: The Women's Legal Education and Action Fund and the Pursuit of Equality*. Toronto: Second Story Press.

———. 1994. "What is to Be Gained by Looking White People in the Eye? Culture, Race, and Gender in Cases of Sexual Violence." *Signs* 19, 4 (Summer), 894–923.

Richter-Lyonette, Elenor. 1998. "Women After the Genocide in Rwanda." In Elenor Richter-Lyonette (ed.), *In the Aftermath of Rape: Women's Rights, War Crimes and Genocide*. Geneva: The Coordination of Women's Advocacy, 101–5.

Ringer, Fritz. 1997. *Max Weber's Methodology*. Cambridge: Harvard University Press.

Rousseau, Stephanie. 1997. "The International Criminal Court for Rwanda: Justice in a Post—but not so Post—Conflict Situation." Paper presented at the Women in Conflict Zones Network workshop, Toronto, May 31–June 1.

Russell, Diana E.H. 1975. *The Politics of Rape: The Victim's Perspective*. New York: Stein and Day.

———. 1982. *Rape in Marriage*. New York: MacMillan.

———. 1993a. "Introduction." In Diana E.H. Russell (ed.), *Making Violence Sexy: Feminist Views on Pornography*. Buckingham: Open University Press, 1–20.

———. 1993b. "From Witches to Bitches: Sexual Terrorism Begets Thelma and Louise." In Diana E.H. Russell (ed.), *Making Violence Sexy: Feminist Views on Pornography*. Buckingham: Open University Press, 254–69.

Sanday, Peggy Reeves. 1990. *Fraternity Gang Rape: Sex, Brotherhood, and Privilege on Campus*. New York: New York University Press.

Scruton, Roger. 1983. *A Dictionary of Political Thought*. London: Pan Books.

Sexwale, Bunie M. Matlanyane. 1994. "Violence Against Women: Experiences of South African Domestic Workers." In Haleh Afshar Mary and Maynard (eds.), *The Dynamics of 'Race' and Gender: Some Feminist Interventions*. London: Taylor and Francis, 196–221.

Sheehey, Elizabeth. 1999. "Legal Responses to Violence Against Women in Canada." *Canadian Women's Studies//Les Cahiers de la Femme* 19, 1/2 (Spring/Summer), 62–73.

Sheffield, Carole J. 1987. "Sexual Terrorism: The Social Control of Women." In Beth B. Hess and Myra Marx Ferree (eds.), *Analyzing Gender: A Handbook of Social Science Research*. Newbury Park: Sage Publications, 171–89.

Smart, Carol. 1989. *Feminism and the Power of Law*. London: Routledge.

———. 1995. *Law, Crime and Sexuality: Essays in Feminism*. London: Sage Publications.

Smith, Dorothy E. 1988. *The Everyday World as Problematic*. Milton Keynes: Open University Press.

Smyth, Ailbhe. 1996. "Seeing Red: Men's Violence Against Women in Ireland." In Chris Corrin (ed.), *Women in a Violent World: Feminist Analyses and Resistance Across 'Europe'*. Edinburgh: Edinburgh University Press, 53–78.

Stanko, Elizabeth A. 1985. *Intimate Intrusions: Women's Experience of Male Violence*. London: Routledge and Kegan Paul.

Stiglmayer, Alexandra. 1994. "The Rapes in Bosnia-Herzegovina." In Alexandra Stiglmayer (ed.), *Mass Rape: The War Against Women in Bosnia-Herzegovina*.

Lincoln: University of Nebraska Press, 82–169.

Stoltenberg, John. 1993. "Pornography and Freedom." In Diana E.H. Russell (ed.), *Making Violence Sexy: Feminist Views on Pornography*. Buckingham: Open University Press, 65–77.

Theweleit, Klaus. 1987. *Male Fantasies Volume I: Women, Floods, Bodies, History*. Cambridge: Polity Press.

Tompkins, Tamara L. 1995. "Prosecuting Rape as a War Crime: Speaking the Unspeakable." *Notre Dame Law Review* 70, 4, 845–90.

Walby, Sylvia. 1989. "Theorising Patriarchy." *Sociology* 23, 2 (May), 213–34.

West, Candace, and Sarah Fenstermaker. 1995. "Doing Difference." *Gender and Society* 9, 1 (February), 8–37.

Wilson, Margo, and Martin Daly. 1992. "Till Death Do Us Part." In Jill Radford and Diana E.H. Russell (eds.), *Femicide: The Politics of Woman Killing*. Buckingham: Open University Press, 83–98.

g, Adrien Katherine, and Sylke Merchán. 1993. "Rape, Ethnicity and Culture: Spirit Injury From Bosnia to Black America." *Columbia Human Rights Law Review* 25, 1, 1–48.

nkler, Cathy, with Penelope J. Hanke. 1995. "Ethnography of the Ethnographer." In Caroline Nordstrom and Antonius C.G.M. Robben (eds.), *Fieldwork Under Fire: Contemporary Studies of Violence and Survival*. Berkeley: University of California Press, 155–85.

Wyre, Ray. 2000. "Paedophile Characteristics and Patterns of Behaviour: Developing and Using a Typography." In Catherine Itzin (ed.), *Home Truths About Child Sexual Abuse: Influencing Policy and Practice, A Reader*. London: Routledge, 49–60.